TWAYNE'S WORLD AUTHORS SERIES

A Survey of the World's Literature

Sylvia E. Bowman, Indiana University

GENERAL EDITOR

NIGERIA

Joseph Jones, University of Texas

EDITOR

Amos Tutuola

(TWAS 62)

TWAYNE'S WORLD AUTHORS SERIES (TWAS)

The purpose of TWAS is to survey the major writers —novelists, dramatists, historians, poets, philosophers, and critics—of the nations of the world. Among the national literatures covered are those of Australia, Canada, China, Eastern Europe, France, Germany, Greece, Italy, Japan, Latin America, New Zealand, Poland, Russia, Scandinavia, Spain, and the African nations, as well as Hebrew, Yiddish, and Latin Classical literature. This survey is complemented by Twayne's United States Authors Series and English Authors Series.

The intent of each volume in these series is to present a critical-analytical study of the works of the writer; to include biographical and historical material that may be necessary for understanding, appreciation, and critical appraisal of the writer; and to present all material in clear, concise English—but not to vitiate the scholarly content of the work by doing so.

Amos Tutuola

By HAROLD R. COLLINS
Kent State University

Twayne Publishers, Inc.   ::   New York

For A. E. C.

Preface

Amos Tutuola's ghost novels certainly deserve more extended treatment than could be given them in articles, reviews of his novels,
and chapters in books on the new African writers. The time has come
to build upon such excellent foundations as Gerald Moore's "Amos
Tutuola: Nigerian Visionary" (*Black Orpheus,* No. 1) and the Tutuola chapter in his *Seven African Writers,* and Ezekiel Mphahlele's
remarks on Tutuola in *The African Image.*

Although critical distortions—due to the West African critics'
hypersensitive pride, and the British and American critics' ignorance
of African conditions and of the feelings of educated Africans—
obscure the situation, the very fact of the emergence of an Afro-
English literature raises literary questions of great interest. Even if
students of literature are not prepared to take Tutuola seriously as a
novelist, or fiction writer, as his compatriots and other West Africans
have often not been, they cannot deny the great importance of the
problems in literary theory raised by Tutuola's work, simply as a
literary phenomenon.

What should a Nigerian English language for serious fiction be
like? Surely not a complete copy of British, or American, English; but
should it be as non-standard as pidgin? (A dramatic group at Ibadan
University has experimented with the use of pidgin for minor characters; this device was found to be quite effective.) Or as Tutuola's
strange English? This question is of practical concern for the criticism of Afro-English literature. For instance, in his "Beginnings of
a Nigerian Literature in English" (April, 1962), Martin Banham
complains of the Americanisms in the novels of Cyprian Ekwensi.
Should Nigerian novels eschew Americanisms? Nigerianisms?

What should be the relations of the rich oral literatures of the
African tribes to the new African literature in English? The characters of the novels of Chinua Achebe are continually quoting Ibo
proverbs and referring to Ibo folk tales. But are such references,
enriching as they are, all that the oral literatures can contribute?

Is Tutuola's gathering together of the tales and making episodic romances out of them really a quite unacceptable, "backward" use of the folk riches?

What mode of fiction, realistic, symbolical, fantastic, or whatever, is appropriate for Nigerian or other West African literatures in English? Is the romance form (at least the romance form as Tutuola writes it, call it the mythical romance) too old-fashioned? Is the realistic novel about contemporary social relations absolutely *de rigueur?*

How should the European novel tradition influence the developing Nigerian novel and what forms of literary acculturation should be encouraged? Are Tutuola's steam-blowing and light-flashing monsters, his Super Lady with the bathroom and dressing room, and his Methodist bishop cousin in the Bush of Ghosts admirable syncretic creations or merely curious?

And most painfully pertinent to the West African critics, how should the modern Nigerian novel come to terms with the African past, especially the "superstitions" and the atrocities? Should the novel accept them all practically without comment, crowding in the most irrational beliefs, the most superstitious observances, and the worst horrors, as Tutuola does? Should it idealize the African past as Chinua Achebe does in *Things Fall Apart* (1958), with a certain nostalgia for the securities and warm ties of the old order before the breaking of the tribes? Or should it self-consciously glory in the African past, as the Négritude poets of the French West Indies and French West Africa do?

And one last simple bread-and-butter question with important literary implications: for whom are the Nigerian novelists writing? In a review of Achebe's *No Longer at Ease* (1960) Omidiji Aragbabalu complains that in Achebe's previous novel "one had occasionally the feeling that here was a Nigerian *explaining* his way of life to Europeans." But if many of his readers are Europeans and Americans . . . ?

The romances of Amos Tutuola of Abeokuta in western Nigeria have put criticism on its mettle. These strange works, strange alike in their merits and their shortcomings, have taken criticism aback both in the West and in Nigeria, producing a kind of misinformed, surprised delight in the West and (usually) shocked anger and bewilderment in Nigeria. But criticism learns new insights when it is puzzled; in the problematical it is shaken out of routine thinking. This study will of course single out for praise the praiseworthy qualities of Tutuola's romances, but probably more important, it will notice the critical adjustments that a sound judgment on the romances requires, and certain relations between his romances and social conditions in Nigeria, and for this purpose it will take up a number of objections raised against Tutuola's work in West Africa. John V. Murra, in his sympathetic review of *The Palm-Wine Drinkard* and *My Life in the Bush of Ghosts* (September, 1954), conveniently summarizes the complaints of educated West Africans to Tutuola's work. The complaints are those mentioned in the text, together with a complaint against obscurity, which really does not seem worth bothering with: the obscurity in Tutuola is quite negligible. These hostile reactions of educated West Africans have furnished us with our points of discussion. Although the response of Western critics was right in the main, it was somewhat uncritical, as though they were bowled over by the strange manner and the subject matter of Tutuola's romances. On the other hand, the unfavorable response of the West Africans, though substantially wrong, raised most of the right critical issues. So this response will structure this study of the romances of Amos Tutuola: *The Palm-Wine Drinkard* (1952), *My Life in the Bush of Ghosts* (1954), *Simbi and the Satyr of the Dark Jungle* (1955), *The Brave African Huntress* (1958), and *Feather Woman of the Jungle* (1962).

A word about Tutuola's latest romance, *Ajaiyi and His Inherited Poverty*, published too late for consideration in this study. It's the mixture as before and of the same high quality. In a quest of considerable ironical piquancy and some contemporary relevance, a gentle and honorable hero-narrator very much like Amos Tutuola, accompanied first by a beloved sister and later by two friends, goes searching for Money, either by well-paid job or by bonanza. Besides various contretemps—among them being forced to "pawn" himself for debts, being kidnapped and almost sacrificed to an "idol," almost being eaten by a "dead-body eating creature" who lives in a pond, being threatened by Spirit of Fire (who's put in his place by Goddess of River), being kept in peonage by a "chairwoman of the witches," and being cheated by a hometown witch doctor—Ajaiyi is repeatedly frustrated in his quest. At the Creator's town he is told that money problems are none of its affair, that only methods of avoiding sin are within its province, and that the Devil handles money troubles: The God of Iron (obviously the Yoruba god Ogun) not only does not give the money-seekers money but burdens them with troublesome talking lumps of iron; the Devil offers lots of money, but at a price the hero is quite properly unwilling to pay. Finally taking his "chronic poverty" back home with him, the gentle hero gains a modest competence from a chain of churches that he has founded with money he has taken from the crooked witch doctor. The point of the long-frustrated quest is clear: the ruler of this fallen world is the Devil; you can get money, "the father of all evils and the creator of all insincerities of this world," but only by paying the price of a short life, "sparing" one dear to you, and promising to be cruel to the righteous.

This romance, like the others, is based on folk materials, such as the underwater goddess and the witch mother who changes into the *pupil of a man's eye*. As usual, there is syncretism with Western elements, especially the myths of popular Christianity in the Africanized account of heaven and the initiation ceremony for the Devil's new followers. The Creator's town, rather like a posh resort area, complete with riding horses (and other riding animals), has a hotel with a plate glass viewing window, where the hero-narrator observes corrupt judges, murderers, liars, "deceivers," and embezzling politicians in the "big flame," and a hall where a corps of drummers glorify the Creator: The bureaucratic methods of the town are probably those of a Nigerian government office. The splendid diabolic initiation ritual, to which the money-seekers ride on a unicorn that "gloats" at them, is graced with the black-robed Devil, his fifty black-robed "disciples," and an "Augur" with an African-style bell.

The language of the new romance is still pure Tutuolan—unschoolmastered and unedited, robust and sinewy—though with a bit more "gravityness" to it than usual and more of the "bad" fragments that require the reader to learn period-hopping.

Perhaps some of Tutuola's less captious critics will note that the plot is not overcrowded with incidents, that the conversational exchanges are more limber than usual (with the usual great battle-boasts and harangues), that more Nigerian customs and beliefs are visible, that the moral orientation is not "mythological" or pagan but clearly Christian. This last romance surely gives this critic no cause to recant. Tutuola is still Tutuola, a classic in world literature.

My thanks are due to a number of persons who helped me in the writing of this study. Ulli Beier, that matchless interpreter of the Nigerian arts, has answered many a query and sent valuable materials from Africa. Mr. Alan Pringle, an editor of Faber and Faber, has been most helpful, especially in providing information on Tutuola's life and his publication plans. Mr. Bernth Lindfors of Los

Angeles, one of the most knowledgeable of American literary Africanists, has read the manuscript and made a number of corrections and most helpful suggestions.

I have benefited from discussions of Nigerian literature with Prof. Martin Banham, at the time of the School of Drama of the University of Ibadan. I have had an interesting and informative correspondence with that brilliant critic of Africa's men of letters, Gerald Moore, at the time Director of Extramural Studies, Makerere University College at Kampala, Uganda.

I appreciate very much the quarter's released time that Kent State University gave me to work on this book and the University Research Committee's help with the cost of typing the manuscript. Mrs. Diane Woolard was good enough to type the bibliography for me with all its formidable African names. But most of all, I am grateful for the unfailing encouragement and sympathetic understanding of my wife, Ethel, who has smoothed the way for all my Africanist labors. Without her help this study never would have been written.

HAROLD R. COLLINS

Kent State University
Kent, Ohio

Contents

Chronology

1920   Amos Tutuola born, Abeokuta, Nigeria; father, Charles Tutuola, a cocoa farmer.

1932   Entered Salvation Army School, Abeokuta; began work as houseboy with F. O. Mornu, civil servant from Ibo tribe.

1934   When Mornu was transferred to Lagos, moved there with his patron and lived in the house of a friend of Mornu's. Started attending Lagos High School. As houseboy was badly mistreated by Mornu's friend's wife.

1936   Discouraged by his troubles with Mornu's friend's wife, did not return to school after December holidays. Returned to Salvation Army School, Abeokuta.

1938   Started attending Anglican Central School, Abeokuta.

1939   Father died. Amos withdrew from school because no relative could afford to pay his tuition fees; tried farming to earn money for fees, but failed because of a drought.

1940   Went to Lagos, living with his brother. Began to learn blacksmithing.

1942   Joined RAF as blacksmith.

1945   Discharged from RAF as grade two blacksmith. Tried to establish blacksmith shop; failed for lack of funds.

1946   Found employment as messenger in Department of Labour, Lagos. Wrote his first romance, *The Palm-Wine Drinkard*.

1947   Married Victoria Alake.

1952   Publication of *The Palm-Wine Drinkard* by Faber and Faber.

1954   Publication of *My Life in the Bush of Ghosts*.

1955   Publication of *Simbi and the Satyr of the Dark Jungle*.

1957   Transferred to Nigerian Broadcasting Corporation, Ibadan. Employed as storekeeper.

1958   Worked with Professor Collis of the University of Ibadan, writing play version of *The Palm-Wine Drinkard*. Publication of *The Brave African Huntress*.

1962   Publication of Gerald Moore's *Seven African Writers,* which contains first readily accessible significant criticism of Tutuola's work. Publication of *Feather Woman of the Jungle.* Staging of the Yoruba version of Tutuola's play *The Palm-Wine Drinkard* in the Arts Theatre, University of Ibadan, in other places in Nigeria, and at the University of Ghana.

1967   Publication of *Ajaiyi and His Inherited Poverty.*

CHAPTER 1

Amos Tutuola: The Shy Yoruba

IN 1920 Amos Tutuola was born in Abeokuta, a large town in the Western Region of Nigeria, about sixty miles north of Lagos, the federal capital. Amos's father, Charles Tutuola (the family name is pronounced approximately as spelled, with the accent on the "o"), was a farmer, with cocoa groves (Abeokuta is in the cocoa belt of Western Region.) Both parents were Christians. As a child at home Amos used to love to listen to his mother's and his aunt's traditional stories, which they had learnt from their mother. At the age of ten young Amos entered the Salvation Army School of Abeokuta. Apparently his father was not very prosperous at the time: an uncle, Mr. Folarin Daley, who was a male nurse at Abeokuta's General Hospital, paid his tuition fees and gave him money for school supplies. At this school he was not a particularly promising student, perhaps because he kept longing for the holidays, when he could go home and work and play on his father's farm, and, best of all, enjoy with his friend, in the cool of the evening, what he was later to call the "plays and amusements" of Abeokuta: "Fables, folk-lores, riddles, etc., etc." [1]

I Schooling and Early Occupations

In 1932 came a kind of crisis in Amos's educational career, an educational career which reminds us of the trials and tribulations, the plucky courage and resourceful persistence, of the heroes and heroines of his folk novels. His mother and his aunt, as anxious as they were for him to go on with his schooling, simply could not afford to feed and clothe the boy and keep him in school. Luckily they managed to find a government clerk, named F. O. Mornu, a friend of the helpful uncle, who was willing to pay for Amos's school tuition and supplies in return for domestic service; that is, Amos became his "houseboy." Every Saturday Amos would go into the "far bush" for firewood, to save his employer the expense of buying it. Mr. Mornu enrolled him in Central School, an Anglican establishment. We do not know why the change was made, but Amos was a better student in this school: he got a double promotion from Infant Class I to Standard I and had had the highest grades in his class.

In 1934 Mr. Mornu was transferred to Lagos, the largest and most westernized city in Nigeria. Amos went with him, because he had been so kind, and enrolled in Lagos High School. Life was hard for Amos in those days. Mr. Mornu and Amos lived in the house of a friend of Mr. Mornu's in crowded Lagos. The school was a mile away, and the wife of Mr. Mornu's friend acted as a sort of fairytale stepmother to Amos. He went off to school every day without a breakfast or pocket money. While the rest of the boys went out to get food during recess, Amos would review his lessons of the morning. Worse yet, the woman kept Amos busy with housework until nine, when she knew his school started at eight. In spite of these deplorable conditions he worked hard and did well in this school. In 1934 he was promoted to Standard II, and in 1935 he got another double promotion, to Standard IV, and was offered a year of schooling free of charge. In 1936 he won promotion to Standard V. But in this year he did not return to Lagos and his school after his December holidays. He simply could not bear any longer the petty tyranny of the wife of his employer's friend.

Perhaps Amos's father was better off by now, because when Amos went to school in Abeokuta again, at the Salvation Army School, his father paid his fees and other school expenses. Amos was in this school about a year, and here he was promoted to Standard VI, in 1937. In January of the next year he transferred to Central School, where he was promoted to Form I. But early in 1939 Amos's father died, and he had to drop out of school, for no one in his family could afford to pay his school expenses. That year Amos tried farming to make money for school fees, but the rains failed that season, his crops failed, and he had to give up hope of going on with his education.

In 1939 he went back to Lagos, this time to learn the trade of blacksmithing, living with his brother in the crowded and expensive city. In 1942 he joined the RAF as a blacksmith. He enjoyed smithery and took a kind of artist's pleasure in bending and shaping the metals; he even thought of setting up in the blacksmithing business for himself after the war. But when he tried to set up a workshop, he found that he needed capital for equipment, and there was no one to lend him money. Giving up the idea of working for himself

he started looking for a job at a very bad time: the horde of soldiers thrown on the labor market had taken most of the jobs, and there were waiting lists. Finally, in 1946, after about a year of unemployment, Amos became a messenger in the Labour Department in Lagos.

II *Beginnings of Writing Career*

And now the story takes a bizarre turn almost suggestive of the hairbreadth escapes and magical transformations of Tutuola's folk novels. In his messenger job, bored and weary of time and clock-watching as he waited for errands, he reverted to his childhood habit of story telling. But since story telling of the usual oral variety is not encouraged in even the most permissive government offices, he wrote his stories on scrap paper. His comment on his first written story, "The Wild Hunter of the Bush of Ghosts," indicates the casual, time-killing purpose of this writing, in the beginning of the most famous writing career in Nigeria: "In a day I cannot sit down doing nothing. I was just playing at it. My intention was not to send it to anywhere." [2]

At this point, Tutuola read in a local paper the advertisement of a bookselling firm specializing in missionary books, and thought the books offered for sale were a publisher's list. He was bitten by that terrible bug, the desire to see his name in print. A few days before, he had written, in a two-day burst of work, his now famous *The Palm-Wine Drinkard*. Deciding that he would offer it to the bookselling firm, for three months he revised and enlarged this work, then sent off the manuscript to The United Society for Christian Literature. This organization, after explaining to Tutuola that it did not publish books, offered to help him find a publisher. Presumably the company sent this extraordinary romance of old-African nightmares to Faber and Faber. At any rate, that distinguished publishing house brought the book out in 1952—and Anglo-Nigerian literature was on the world scene, for it was immediately successful. All honor to those anonymous missionary booksellers whose bold, unconventional (and sound) literary taste, breadth of sympathy, and true Christian kindliness enriched English literature.

In spite of the astonishing success of *The Palm-Wine Drinkard*, Tutuola had at first no intention of becoming a professional writer. He still wanted to be a blacksmith. But though he had passed a trade test, he could not get a job in that trade. Perhaps at this time he needed more money to support his wife and mother (he had married Victoria Alake in 1947), or perhaps he felt some sort of artistic compulsion. At any rate, he started *My Life in the Bush of Ghosts*. Again the writing was done in a two-day burst of work and three months of revision. (Like D. H. Lawrence, Tutuola revises, not by minutely tinkering with the text, but by rewriting those passages which do not convey adequately the inner vision.) *My Life in the Bush of Ghosts* was almost as successful as the previous book, and Tutuola, the shy junior clerk, was established as a genuine West African literary bombshell.[3]

The reception accorded Tutuola's first two books in Nigeria, England, and America is as strange as the circumstances of their writing. In England he was a big success; his books got enthusiastic reviews from Dylan Thomas and V. S. Pritchett. In America Grove Press brought out his second romance, and he achieved such fame as to be mentioned in *Vogue*. French, German, Italian, and Yugoslav translations attested to considerable European interest.[4] Later, in 1963, the West German government offered Tutuola a scholarship to visit Germany for nine months. (He never went.)

III *Reception of First Work in Nigeria*

But a prophet can be without honor even in dynamic, increasingly literate Nigeria. Many educated Nigerians were simply horrified by the books. They deplored his "crudities," his lack of inhibitions, and the folk tale basis of his romances (too commonplace for their tastes and allegedly plagiarized from printed collections); they accused poor, shy, diffident Tutuola of encouraging an unprogressive kind of mythical thinking, of leading West African literature up a blind alley, and, most important, of giving the supercilious, prejudiced westerners an excuse for continuing to patronize the allegedly superstitious Nigerians! The Nigerians' sense of their vulnerability to western scorn seems to give the greatest force to their objections to Tutuola's work. This sense of vulnerability appears, for instance, in Mr. Adeagbo Akinjogbin's letter to the editor of *West Africa* of June 5, 1954.[5] Mr. Akinjogbin complains that "most Englishmen, as perhaps Frenchmen, are pleased to believe all sorts of fantastic tales about Africa, a continent about which they know they are profoundly ignorant," and that Tutuola's books, because they contain "some of the unbelievable things in our folklores," are calculated to cater to the "temper of his European readers as they seem to confirm their concept of Africa." Since Tutuola is "not an academic man" (!) it simply must be something besides a "high literary standard that has attracted so many European and American readers." Mr. Akinjogbin confesses that he has not himself read Tutuola's "extraordinary books," but he "gathers" that they have no literary value and "show no mark of possible future development."

A most thoroughgoing attack from a Mr. Babasola Johnson in a letter to the editor of *West Africa* of April 10, 1954 is representative.[6] Mr. Johnson says flatly that *Drinkard* should not have been published at all. The language of the book is "foreign to West Africans and English people, or anybody for that matter." Mr. Johnson would not have approved of "an African narrative" in "good English," but such a narrative in Tutuola's "strange lingo" is inexcusable. Tutuola's language "consists largely in translating Yoruba ideas into English," together with the "inclusion of words taken from the dictionary at random." Mr. Johnson calls into question Tutuola's originality, maintaining that the episodes of *Drinkard* have been "published in one form or another," and that Tutuola has borrowed extensively from Mr. Fagunwa's Yoruba tale *Ogboju Ode*.

A letter to the editor of *West Africa* of May 8, 1954 [7] from Miss Mercedes Mackay, a West Indian writer, reveals some of the motivation for the furor about Tutuola's work. After noting that many Africans agree with Mr. Johnson in deprecating the high praise given Tutuola and reminding her readers that much West African writing has been wooden and stilted in its lifeless correctness, she makes a shrewd observation: "The translation of well known and rather horrific folk stories into ungrammatical and incomprehensible English [much exaggerated, this charge of obscurity] is naturally shocking to an African (or European) who has labored with his grammar and got prizes for his essays at school . . . ." Miss Mackay admits that Tutuola's work has the spontaneity essential to good art and she makes a very astute judgment on Tutuola's maverick manner when she says that "a writer that has no grammar just does without; but the flow and the colour and the rhythm remain, even if some comprehension is lost." As we shall see when we come to consider in more detail the language of Tutuola's works, some Nigerian critics recognized Tutuola's extraordinary talent, but Tutuola has always been "controversial," and even now a Westerner's praise for Tutuola will bring a somewhat wary glance from an educated Nigerian.

And it must be admitted that the Western critics' admiration for Tutuola's work was pretty much of a flash in the pan. After *My Life in the Bush of Ghosts* these critics are either silent or patronizingly severe or damningly faint in their praise. Ann Tibble's account of the reception of his later books is probably as accurate as it is silly-sounding: the critics, she says, thought that the "magic" had "leaked away." For instance, there is the *Times Literary Supplement* reviewer who sourly complains that "it is pointless to look for any exact symbolism" in the "primary colours," the "mixture of sophistication, superstition, and primitivism" of *Feather Woman of the Jungle;* anyway the earlier interest in Tutuola was an affair of "novelty-seekers, propagandists for the coloured races, and rooters for the Avant Garde." A reviewer of *Feather Woman* in *The Spectator* pontificates that Tutuola's naïveté is no longer "pleasingly childlike" but is now "deliberately childish"; and urges him to find a "more mature means of expression for his undoubted powers of imagination." A *New Statesman* review of the same romance is avuncularly forgiving. Although the naïveté "tarnished" in Tutuola's later books and they were rather less successful, this last work shows signs that the author has learned that "certain western tricks of presentation are worth picking up." A *New York Times* reviewer calls *The Brave African Huntress* unsuccessful because Tutuola has not "learned to communicate" and because his mythologies do not "relate to anything in our mythology, or to other mythologies with which we are familiar." And yet Tutuola continues to have readers in this country, and Anne Tibble reports that British libraries have his books and that they get read.[8]

IV   *Later Career*

In 1956 Tutuola got a job slightly more suitable for a well-known author; he became a storekeeper for the Nigerian Broadcasting Corporation at Lagos, and has since risen to the senior grade in this rather modest work. In 1957 he arranged to have himself transferred to the Ibadan offices of the N.B.C., wanting to move to Ibadan so that he could work with Professor Collis of the University of Ibadan, an admirer of his books, who helped him write a play version of *The Palm-Wine Drinkard,* later translated into Yoruba. This folk drama version in Yoruba, produced with considerable acclaim at the University of Ibadan Arts Theatre, in Ghana, and in various theaters throughout Nigeria, has done a good deal to win over Tutuola's compatriots. Indeed, by now, most educated Nigerians are willing to admit that American and English critics may just possibly be right, that Tutuola is in fact a great writer. As is entirely proper, Tutuola is a charter member of the Mbari Club, the writers' and publishers' organization of Ibadan, and first-hand reports from those familiar with Mbari Club indicate that he is by all odds the shyest and most self-effacing member.[9]

News of this extremely modest man is hard to come by. He now has two children. The Nigerian novelist Cyprian Ekwensi has told this writer that Tutuola's extreme simplicity makes him the despair of interviewers. Tutuola simply cannot talk in the fashionable literary patois of our time; nor is he the sort of person to attend publishers' parties, go on lecture tours, or hobnob with fellow-writers. As a writer he is very isolated: his background is quite different from that of his fellow-writers in Nigeria, most of them university graduates who have traveled overseas and now hold positions in the higher ranks of government service. In such circumstances the readers of the English-speaking world have cause to be thankful that Tutuola's independence of spirit and wonderful assurance have sustained him in a very strange writing career.

"Nigerian Correspondent" of *West Africa* found him "shyly polite" and "slow and diffident" in speech, but again we may wonder if the manner were not largely due to the strange company. Would he be as reserved with the "tailors, blacksmiths, carpenters, and other tradesmen," many of them illiterate, with whom he spent so many evenings about the time he was writing his first two novels? His letters give the impression, not so much of reserve or shyness, but of quiet dignity; he seems a gentle soul of great simplicity.

Tutuola looks rather like some of our Afro-Americans (not surprising, since many of our black Americans have Yoruba ancestors). "Nigerian Correspondent" calls his face "homely" (ordinary? unpretentious?) and notices his pleasant smile. His photographs show an engaging open expression of face and a rather distinguished-looking high forehead. Probably if we were walking about in a big Nigerian government office, like the Nigerian Broadcasting Company's, where he works, we would scarcely notice Amos Tutuola. The "Nigerian Correspondent" says he looks like "a thousand other junior government clerks" [10]—a thought which gives pause: we wonder if many other minor government clerks have compelling fantasies like those of Tutuola.

Judging from the ghost novels, Amos Tutuola still loves to listen to the old people telling the traditional tales. But he also enjoys western literary fare; he reads newspapers, pictorial magazines, and books. Eric Larrabee has reported that he enjoyed Joyce Cary's *Mister Johnson* (about a fictional junior government clerk) and Edith Hamilton's *Mythology*,[11] which has a lot of tales very like his

own episodes in the novels. He reads technical books; at one time
he was trying to procure J. R. Eaton's *Beginning Electricity* and
Alfred Morgan's *The Boy's First Book of Radio and Electronics*.[12]
And he enjoys writing, or perhaps he is driven to write. Ibadan
literary gossip has it that he writes constantly, mostly late at night.
According to the *West Africa* interviewer, Tutuola has confessed
that "he more than half-believes the tales that he writes and he can,
without mental trauma, reconcile this quasi-belief with his strong
Christian views." [13] This alleged contradiction can be reconciled
rather more easily than the interviewer supposes, as we shall see
when we come to consider the Jungian archetypes in Tutuola's work.

V *Tutuola's Yoruba Background*

And now a word about the land of the Yoruba, Amos Tutuola's
home country. As we have observed, he was born of Christian
parents in the Yoruba city of Abeokuta, Western Region, Nigeria.
The Yoruba peoples may be the largest cultural group in West Africa
with a historical background of political unity. The great Yoruba
state of Oyo arose some time between A. D. 600 and 1000, when
migrants, possibly part Hamites (some Yoruba scholars say from
Upper Egypt) imposed their rule on the ancient civilization of Ile
Ife, which to judge from surviving examples of sculpture in stone
and bronze, had a high level of culture. The center of power in the
Oyo kingdom shifted from Ife to the town of Oyo, but Ife remained
the religious and cultural center: the best bronze work was done
there, and the Sword of Justice used in the investiture of the alafin
of Oyo and of the kings of the smaller successor kingdoms was kept
there. The Yoruba state was the earliest, the largest, the longest-
lasting, and the most prosperous and cultivated of the so-called
forest-states; the others are better known because of certain sensa-
tional characteristics of their nineteenth century history. In the
middle of the eighteenth century, when the Yoruba state reached
the pinnacle of its power, it ruled over an area extending from the
southern bend of the lower Niger to a point south of Abeokuta and
including a good deal of what is now Dahomey. Great power and
wealth came to Oyo, largely because of extensive military operations:
every able-bodied man served in the army, and an army was fielded
every dry season; unsuccessful generals were expected to kill themselves or go into exile.

Although the Oyo kingdom broke up into warring kingdoms and
chiefdoms in the nineteenth century, the Yorubas still feel themselves

to be one people. As Tutuola's king of Ife explains it, in *Feather Woman of the Jungle*, "all Yoruba *obas* [kings] like the Alake of Abeokuta, Alafin of Oyo, Owa of Ilesha, Alaketu of Dahomey, Olubini of Benin, etc. etc. etc. were the sons of Oduduwa," who is "the father of all Yorubas." That is, the original kings of the Oyo state and the successor states were sons of the founding father Oduduwa, a legendary god-king. The Yorubas all worship the same gods, or *orishas*, as they are called. The Yoruba language unites them. There has been considerable intermarriage between members of the various Yoruba kingdoms and chiefdoms.

With the exception of the Efik of Calabar and some of the Ijaw of the Niger Delta, the Yoruba have been subjected to more intense Westernization than any other Nigerian people. Christian missionaries entered Yorubaland in 1841. Lagos, a predominantly Yoruba town, was annexed to the British crown in 1861 and has long been an important gateway to Western influence as Nigeria's principal port and her most important administrative center. One of the two north-south railway trunk lines—the Lagos-Nguru railroad—passes through Yorubaland bringing to the Yoruba the influence of Western-style trade and commerce. Yorubaland produces Nigerian cocoa, one of Nigeria's most important export products. The Yoruba are a very "progressive" people, anxious to be educated, to improve their conditions of life, and to accept the ways and works of the white man.[14] But for all its Western influence Yorubaland has its share of traditional thought and practice. Among western Nigerian towns, Abeokuta is especially noted for its traditional festivals and processions and its interest in traditional lore.

CHAPTER 2

The Ghost Novels as Naive Quest Romances

IT will be possible, at length, to establish Tutuola in the tradition of what Northrop Frye terms "naive quest romance." Before arguing the case for his inclusion in this particular category, however, we may find it useful to examine some of the elements of the separate romances in order to realize more clearly how the designation finally applies. How does the story teller manage such matters as conversation, characterization, plot-structure, and the like?

I *Conversation*

Although educated West Africans may not have noticed such technical curiosities as the very loose episodic structure of Tutuola's first three novels, the lack of well-developed interior views in *Simbi and the Satyr of the Dark Jungle* (the other novels are told in the first person), and the anticlimactic incidents in all but *Simbi and the Satyr of the Dark Jungle*, and *Feather Woman of the Jungle*, they must certainly have noticed his troubles with the management of conversation.

Not until *Simbi and the Satyr of the Dark Jungle* does Tutuola write well-developed scenes with conversational exchanges. *The Palm-Wine Drinkard*, which is written in panoramic narrative, to use Percy Lubbock's term, is particularly crude in this respect: almost all the conversation is given in indirect quotation form with some loss of immediacy. With *My Life in the Bush of Ghosts* Tutuola has improved somewhat his handling of conversation: there arc a few conversational explanations and exclamations in direct quotations and some rather wooden conversational exchanges, like the scene in which Super Lady proposes to the hero.[1] However, with *Simbi and the Satyr of the Dark Jungle* he has achieved a measure of competence: the developed scene in which Dogo the kidnapper and Simbi berate each other, those scenes in which Simbi and the Satyr trade battle boasts, and the chattering of Simbi and her "refugee" friends are spirited and effective, though some of the speech tags might seem a little quaint—"asked wonderfully," "remarked painfully," "perplexly asked," "warned her whisperly." [2] Curiously enough, *The Brave African Huntress* represents a sort of retreat into the straight narrative manner of *The Palm-Wine Drinkard,* with the same overworking of the indirect quotation. But there are two notable exceptions, two fine conversational exchanges: the charming battle-boast scene between Adebesi (the heroine) and the "bad semi-bird" and that between Adebesi and the "huge stern pigmy." [3]

In *Feather Woman of the Jungle* the conversation makes fairly free use of the direct quotation, but there is still a stiffness about the conversational exchanges, a kind of excessive gravity (we are tempted to say in Tutuolan, too much "gravityness") which makes for awkwardness; for instance: "Then with lower voice he asked from her: 'Lady what are you weeping for?' Ashabi replied that: 'I am weeping for my two brothers (she pointed to us and the old man gazed at us (images) with wonder). And I tried all my efforts to change them back to their own forms but all my efforts had failed and I must not return to my father and mother without them.'" The stiffness is not apparent in some of the more passionate conversations, like the outbursts of the Treacherous Queen, the battle boasts of the Hairy Giant, and the cries of the mad man.[4]

II Structure

But for all these defects, Tutuola's ghost novels are fairly competent in construction and characterization. The episodic structures are justified by the tradition in which Tutuola is working: Drinkard's search for his dead tapster friend in Deads' Town is the folklore Quest to the Underworld. This quest involves Drinkard and his wife in "uncountable" ordeals, tribulations, and adventures—mostly preternatural—with such worthies as Death, the Skull, the crazy and cruel creatures of Unreturnable-heaven's Town, Faithful-Mother, the Red-people, the prince-killer, the hostile dead babies, and the hungry-creature. The book ends, not with the discovery of the dead tapster, but with the relief of a famine—a cosmic finale in the tradition of the Yoruba creation myths.

My Life in the Bush of Ghosts describes the hero-narrator's twenty-four years of an odyssey on his way home from the frightful "bad bush" full of odd and usually malevolent spirits (among them Smelling-Ghost, Burglar-Ghosts, and the short ghosts, a flash-eyed mother, Super Lady, and the Television-handed Ghostess). *Simbi and the Satyr of the Dark Jungle* details Simbi's quest for the "poverties and punishments of life."

The Brave African Huntress relates the dauntless heroine's quest for her four hunter brothers who have been killed or "detained" by the hostile pigmies; she means to "kill or drive the whole pigmies away from that jungle" and to kill all the dangerous wild animals. And after being cruelly manhandled by the pigmies, the Brave African Huntress does just that, kills all the wild animals, blows up the pigmy camp, shoots down most of the pigmies, and rescues her brothers, together with some other home village men.

The quest in the *Feather Woman of the Jungle* is the narrator's search for money to relieve the poverty and pay the debts of his parents; the new chief of a village is narrating to his villagers six of his "journeys" or fortune-hunting adventures, in ten "entertainments" or story-telling sessions, accompanied by the Nigerian amenities—dancing and palm-wine drinking. The narrator's adventures with such notables as the Feather Woman, the King of the Bush of Quietness, the savage people, the Queen of the River, the Goddess of the Diamonds, and the Hairy Giant and Giantess are sufficiently exciting and bizarre, but the purpose of the adventures—the quest for fortune—is hardly ever lost sight of.

III *Characterization*

In spite of their simplicity, discussed in another connection, all of Tutuola's principal characters are substantial and credible. (By substantial I mean solidly "there," not dim, or shadowy.) In *The Palm-Wine Drinkard*, in spite of the first-person point of view (which often blurs or blanks out the narrator in fiction) and the awkward conversation, Drinkard is clearly established as a shrewd, witty, easygoing Yoruba. Though his wife does not come through quite so clearly, we do catch a glimpse of the plucky, practical, comradely Nigerian woman of real life, a type that deserves to be better known as one of the most charming varieties of emancipated woman in the modern world. The wanderer in the Bush of Ghosts is very like Drinkard, though he is explicitly distinguished from him. Perhaps he is slightly more credible in that he usually exercises his wit and pluck without benefit of the almost inexhaustible store of juju that Drinkard has at his command. The two (successive) wives of this African Odysseus—the "beautiful ghostess" and Super Lady—are, unlike Drinkard's consort, rather shadowy creatures. But by virtue of the author-omniscient point of view sharply focused on

Simbi, the developed scenes illustrating her qualities, the more plausible "punishments" she suffers, and her human companionship with her "refugee" friends, Simbi is a more substantial and credible character than even Drinkard and the wanderer in the Bush of Ghosts. She is a fictional counterpart of the spunky Nigerian woman of strong initiative and impressive militancy; she reminds us of the Nigerian trading woman, or the big business woman, or the lady passive resister in those Nigerian Women's Wars described in Joyce Cary's *African Witch* (1936). Though Simbi's friends Rali, Sala, and Kadara are "flat" characters without much individuality or literary vitality, her friend Bako, the atrociously pugnacious twin horribly transformed into a "cockish lady," has real, though rather grotesque, individuality. And we might add that the Satyr is a very human— we must really say credible—kind of monster, a kind of noisier, more braggadocio Caliban. Indeed, many of the monsters are entirely substantial and credible as characters. Among other substantial, credible monsters might be mentioned a flash-eyed mother in *My Life in the Bush of Ghosts,* huge stern pigmy in *The Brave African Huntress,* and the Feather Woman, the title character in the fifth romance. These monsters have entirely human attributes; only their appearance and their power is preternatural.[5]

And yet surely Adebesi, the Brave African Huntress, is the most substantial, most credible, and most engaging character in the novels. Perhaps she is so partly because she is sparring with the juju, partly because she has human, though not necessarily cordial, relations with the human pigmies (especially the "gatekeepers" and the keepers of the "custody"), with the bachelors of the womanless town, the old man, and the old man's persecutor, Ajantala: and so is able to show her qualities. At any rate, she has this writer's nomination for the title of the greatest little huntress, female wrestler, and female boxer of Anglo-African literature.[6]

In *Feather Woman of the Jungle* the elder of a Yoruba village, recently chosen chief, who relates the "entertainments," is substantial and credible—both in the time of his story telling and the earlier time of his fortune-hunting. Again the first-person narration has not dimmed the narrator. Like the other first-person narrators in Tutuola's romances, he is a plucky, resourceful hero with considerable sangfroid. Like them he is always pushing ahead in spite of great fear. This narrator's notives are much more commercial than those of Tutuola's other heroes, but he seeks his fortune, not by manufacturing or merchandising (or swindling), but by risking his neck in daring adventures. Perhaps this hero is more sober-sided than the other Tutuola heroes, or it may be that he merely seems so because he is a sixty-year-old chief when he narrates his adventures. (The chief consumes a keg of palm wine at each story telling session.)

There are several rather well-developed female characters in this romance besides the already mentioned Feather Woman: the Treacherous Queen, as skillful in witchcraft as she is disloyal and adulterous; the Queen of the River, a beautiful, intelligent, and rather imperious grand dame of about thirty; and the Goddess of the Diamonds, a bad-tempered and vindictive potentate. (Her daughter Sela is, like the wives of the Wanderer in the Bush of Ghosts, rather dim.)⁷

The characterization in Tutuola's romances suggests a rather bold literary hypothesis: that to be "living" or vital a literary character does not have to be complicated or well developed (i.e., may be what E. M. Forster calls a "flat" character),⁸ or realistic, or even human. Tutuola is a difficult writer for criticism to handle, but as is so often true of problematical subject matters, he occasions new insights into the literary art.

IV *Point of View*

Point of view, or the method by which a novel or short story is told, is always an important consideration in fiction, and Tutuola's romances are particularly interesting in this respect. Both *The Palm-Wine Drinkard* and *My Life in the Bush of Ghosts* are told by first-person hero-narrators—Drinkard and the unnamed wanderer in the Bush of Ghosts. Neither narrator is aware of himself as an amateur or professional writer; each is a voice speaking, uninterrupted, to no particular audience, a voice which the reader overhears, though he is not explicitly addressed. Neither narrator describes his personal appearance or passes along to the reader any other character's description of his appearance. Similarly, neither narrator describes his own personality traits or quotes any other character that does so. (We must bear in mind how difficult it is for a first-person narrator to describe his own looks and personality—especially *favorably*.)

Of course these two narrators do demonstrate such traits as courage, ingenuity, and persistence by what they do and say, and they also tell us explicitly about certain of their feelings, particularly simple ones like pain and fear, as in "I was greatly terrified. . . ." and "I was feeling hunger as if I would die soon." ⁹ But generally the interior views, the insights into the narrators' minds, do not parallel and support the external horrors and ordeals, so that the effect is a kind of dream-like dissociation between experience and feeling tone. And yet, since the narrators' most conspicuous virtues are such simple ones as pluck, steadfastness, and shrewdness, the narrators are solidly and substantially there for us. It seems obvious that these two narrators are reliable; that is, they are not liars, they are not mistaken, and their standards of conduct are acceptable. Of course readers unfamiliar with romance standards of plausibility might need to be told that they should accept the narrators' norms of reality.

Simbi and the Satyr of the Dark Jungle is told in the third-person by what is generally called the omniscient author, but which might be more accurately described as an author's voice, speaking in the third person, a disembodied voice, without any personality, not consciously an author, and usually limiting his narration to the externals of speech and action, only occasionally giving rather clumsy interior views, like "I am entirely fed up with my mother's wealths. I can no longer bear to remain in the happiness . . . ." [10]

The conversational exchanges are more developed in *Simbi,* and they help characterize the heroine, especially her plucky bravura in battle-boasting and monster-fighting. Since *Simbi* is not so crowded with incidents as the two previous romances, each episode is more fully developed with supporting details and functions more effectively for characterization, that is, brings out very clearly the heroine's jaunty courage, resourcefulness, and high good cheer. Simbi is a reliable narrator, within the framework of romance standards of reality.

The Brave African Huntress is told by a first-person narrator-heroine who is unaware of the work of narration and whose appearance is not given by the narrator herself or other characters (although the men of Bachelors' town's "scrambling" for her and pampering her as their queen in the womanless town is a kind of implied description).[11] Neither the narrator herself nor the other characters comment on her personality traits, unless we count the gratitude and the praise of her valor elicited by her killing of the "semi-bird," or the prison warden's realization (reported by the narrator) that she was "smart" and able to serve him "to his entire satisfaction." [12] The heroine demonstrates some of her traits—the courage and resourcefulness, for instance, found in all Tutuola heroes and heroines. Besides being a fearless and tricky monster-and-pigmy fighter, she is a female Robinson Crusoe, as witness her setting up of a refugee camp for men surviving the pigmies' "custody" and her elaborate preparations for the canoe trip home.[13] As in *Simbi* there are not too many incidents for proper development of character, and the Brave African Huntress' exploits with such unworthies as the cudgel-throwing Odara, the "semi-bird," the huge stern pigmy, and the trickster Ajantala work effectively in characterizing the heroine. Like the Drinkard and the wanderer in the Bush of Ghosts, the Brave African Huntress mentions such simple feelings as fear, as in "But after a few seconds his fear [her fear of him] stopped me at a little distance from him," and "I began to sweat and I was trembling with great fear of not being killed by them" (note curious "negative of fear").[14] Sometimes the extent of the fear is indicated rather indirectly, as in the humorous but not very genteel "I feared him so much that I did not know when I opened my mouth and the spit was dropping down." [15]

As with Drinkard and the wanderer, the notations on the narrator's feelings do not seem to square with the external situations. A reader used to the very full accounts of characters' feelings in modern fiction is likely to be a bit taken aback by the odd, matter-of-fact tone, the unnatural sangfroid, illustrated by the following description of the enraged mob lusting after the heroine's blood: "As they were chasing me along to kill and when I believed they would overtake me very soon then I started to shoot them with my gun. But when several of them were wounded then they went back from me." [16] It seems obvious that the Huntress is an entirely reliable narrator: we need not discount in any way what Adebesi says about her adventures, no matter how marvelous they may be (and they are much less marvelous than the adventures of other Tutuola hero-heroines.)

The Feather Woman of the Jungle is told by a first-person narrator, the village chief who tells us how he related to his subjects his six "journeys" or adventures in ten "entertainments" or story-sessions. Since the villagers' comments and reactions are quite perfunctory, the effect is much the same as ordinary first-person narration. A comment like "It was a terrible journey indeed although you had returned with money," or a reaction like "then they shouted with joy" scarcely constitute a choral commentary or qualification of the narrator's presentation.[17] The chief is obviously aware of his village audience (he addresses them often), but hardly of his readers, or of his presentation to readers. The narrator's appearance is not indicated in any way, except that we are given his age at the time of his first adventure, and time signals indicate the time elapsing between adventures. The narrator's traits must be seen in his speech and his actions, mostly his actions, since he is not as voluble as some of Tutuola's heroes and heroines. The situations are sometimes rather more complex in this romance than in the others: being changed into images, helping an enchanted king get release and revenge from his faithless spouse, getting a magic food box from an underwater queen and then—against explicit orders—coming back for a replacement when it is stolen, stealing diamonds and a daughter from a Goddess of Diamonds, sight-seeing among the marvels of the sacred city of the Yorubas—all these activities are less elementary than Tutuola's derring-do with ogres, ghosts, or pigmies. However, even the feelings associated with these somewhat more complex activities are as simple as the situations allow, mostly varieties of fear, pain, surprise, prudent thoughtfulness. The narrator's feelings are, as in the other romances, mentioned explicitly but without much emphasis, or implied in gesture or action as in "After a while I hid my pains," or "I replied with trembling voice." [18] As a character in his own adventures, the chief is not clearly individualized; he is not, like Drinkard, Drinkard's wife, the wanderer, Simbi, the Satyr (!), or the Huntress, a clearly distinct fictional person. The chief is, however, a reliable narrator; his powers owe more to magic than those of the huntress, but we must go by romantic standards of credibility, as we do in the first four romances.

The general effect of Tutuola's first-person narration is hard to describe accurately, but though it tasks one's critical acumen a description must be attempted, for that effect is an important part of Tutuola's characteristic manner. We might note at first that his narrators do not impress us as egoistic introverts; their feelings are too often simplified or even blanked out for that effect, and the emphasis is thrown outward upon the external events—mostly horrors and marvels. And yet the feelings are shown more conspicuously than they would in the so-called dramatic method that limits itself to the externals of speech and action. The feelings are shown, and since they are simple and intense, they tend to leave an impression of inwardness, as it were.[19]

V *Plot Management*

In Tutuola's romances the novel-reader will miss, and probably be uncomfortable in missing, one of several possible orders of progression of the kind we generally call a plot (a chain of incidents linked by consequence, a development of a theme, or a structure of juxtaposed images or symbols). The minor adventures are not arranged in a pattern of increasing excitement, or importance, or even of nearer approach to some goal; as we have indicated before, most of the episodes could be placed somewhere else in the novel. Geoffrey Parrinder was probably thinking of this missing novelistic structuring when he asked Tutuola "the reason for the apparently haphazard order of the towns of the ghosts." Tutuola answered quite simply, "That is the order I came to them." This rather cryptic answer suggests to Parrinder "how deeply he lived in his own narrative," but surely writers of novels with plotted incidents have also "lived deeply in their narratives," Trollope for instance. To Gerald Moore, Tutuola's answer is evidence confirming Moore's notion that Tutuola is a "visionary" rather than a novelist.[20] As we indicated earlier, Tutuola's novels have the episodic structure of the more extended Yoruba folk tales; they are simply extended a little longer.

There are two organizing devices, however, beyond the quest pattern. Gerald Moore has noticed that Tutuola notifies his reader at the very beginning of the story what the quest is to be: "Tutuola . . . understands very well that however he may expand or digress in the body of his story, he must introduce us to the main plot at once." We might add that a careful reading of Tutuola shows that he occasionally reminds us what the "main plot" is. Drinkard's capturing death is supposed to win him news of his dead tapster's whereabouts from the old man; his rescuing his wife-to-be is supposed to gain similar information from her father (he reneges, then finally performs); the people of the town mentioned by the father direct Drinkard to Deads' Town. The prince-killer pretends to give them directions to that place. The prince's father, after almost executing Drinkard and his wife, does actually direct them to Deads' Town. But as a farmer on Wraith-Island, as a free-loader at Faithful-Mother's, as a monster-killer in Red-town, and in a score or more other adventures with monsters and marvels, Drinkard seems to forget his mission to find his dead tapster. Occasionally he wakes up, as it were, in the burgeoning, proliferating mass of nightmarish adventures and resolves to get on with the job: "To go back was harder and to go further was the hardest, so at last we made up our minds and started to go forward." The purposes of returning home and relieving the town's famine with the magic egg and the sacrifice are more easily kept in view, in spite of the assaulting dead babies on the road home, the giant who puts them in a bag with cold, hairy, sandpapery creatures who fight with Drinkard, a "hungry-creature" that swallows Drinkard and his wife and their loads, a stay in a "mixed town" solving judicial dilemmas, an altercation with mountain creatures who pursue Drinkard and his wife to a river's edge, a cosmic quarrel between Land and Heaven, and a riot or two over the miraculous feeding with the magic egg.[21]

My Life in the Bush of Ghosts has its intermittent home thoughts. Although the wanderer in the bush of ghosts, even after he has finished with the copperish, silverish, and golden ghosts, the Smelling-Ghost, and the homeless ghosts, seems in no great hurry to go home or to think of home, we are reminded of the Odyssey motif by his remark, "I did not remember to start to find the way to my home again." His remembering and his forgetting of home, both duly reported, remind us. For three months of his first marriage, he tells us, he has forgotten about his mother and brother. After the long ordeal as a long-necked, swivel-eyed god in a jug, he once more starts "to wander about searching for the way to my home town as usual." After the harrowing experiences with the talking bush, the spider-eating ghosts, the blowing bush, the monumental woman-hill with the thousands of baby heads and her short ghost cohorts, and the creatures "barbing" with "clippers and knife of fire," the narrator's mind is "not at rest to live there any longer except to continue to look for the way to my home town . . . ." Looking hard for the way home, he meets his second wife-to-be, Super Lady, and we hear nothing about home thoughts while we read of his good times with the lovely Westernized Lagos-style beauty in Nameless-town (an all-woman town) and Hopeless-town (where the inhabitants talk in shrugs). However, when the two quarrel, and the Super Lady drives him out of town, the narrator remembers "to continue to be looking for the way to my home town as I had forgotten that for a while, because of love."

After becoming a kind of naturalized ghost, speaking fluent ghost language, being ridden by a ghost for three days, arrested for burglary in a town where they worship mosquitoes, and sentenced to sixteen years in a charcoal oven (which he stokes himself in the night time!), he is rescued by the king of the town—who turns out to be his son by Super Lady. Having stayed with this king for *several years* he thinks of home again and asks the king to "show him the way to go home," as the song says. The king can't tell him; telling would be against the rules of the Bush of Ghosts. In the fourth town of ghosts the king offers to tell him the way to the nearest earthly town if he will "volunteer" his left arm. After the wanderer has performed a suitable substitute service for this king, the king reneges on his promise. Following the long account of the "Christianity works" of his dead cousin we hear that he wishes to live with the cousin "for a short period to rest for some time for all the punishment . . . and then to continue to find the way as before." During the "short period" he learns to read and write, studies "the law and police work," sets up court and police systems, and becomes chief justice before he is brought home (though not without further painful adventures) by the agency of the fortune-teller's "magnetic missive" and the Television-handed Ghostess' magic TV screen in her palm and is reunited with his brother and mother so that "Gladness becomes Weeping." [22]

Simbi and the Satyr of the Dark Jungle is probably the most tightly organized of the romances. Since there are not a great number of episodes, the romance does not seem congested; the incidents do not overwhelm the reader's attention, as they sometimes do in the first two books. Although Simbi's original quest is her search for "the poverties and the punishments" of life, from the moment of her first experience of these formidable conditions, when the slaver Dogo captures her, she is really seeking her way home. She and her friends are always trying to find the "right path that leads to [their] village." [23] There are enough references to their search for the path to convince the reader that they genuinely want to get home as soon as they can. [24]

The episodes of the romance are, as in the *Odyssey*, so many delays and obstacles in this homeward progress. The delaying and obstructing episodes do not seem arbitrary; given the standards of credibility of the romantic mode of fiction, they seem quite credible. And the episodes are absorbing. What reader could, momentarily, care if Simbi *ever* gets home while she is living so dangerously and, for us, so entertainingly as when she sings her "kind of a melodious song" and sets her executioners to dancing, and then beheads a king, or when she in five wild encounters, boxes, wrestles, and bandies magic with the Satyr, or when she sings and dances in the Satyr's "illusive hall," built of migratory birds and featuring a variously visible orchestra (hands only showing, or faces or bodies), "ultra-beautiful" girls and white-shoed ostriches? [25] Sometimes, and this is as it should be, the reader cannot imagine how Simbi will ever get home, as when her mad friend Bako steals the old woman's hen in the town of the "multi-coloured" people who are so suspicious of "mono-coloured" persons, or when she falls down inside the hollow tree under the eagle's nest, or when the Satyr's "assistance," "the Phoenix bird" is swooping down on her and her friends and dropping stones on them.[26]

On two occasions Simbi may appear to linger unnecessarily on her homeward journey. In the town of the multi-coloured people, when the king insists that Simbi and her friends find work in the village, Simbi plants crops, which suggests she means to stay quite a while. But the reader should reflect that farming is the only work available to a woman in her wayfaring condition. When the wood-cutter rescues Simbi from the hollow tree she is willing to marry him only after his promise that he will show her the way home in "a few months." Not until she has had two babies by him and lost them both by ritual sacrifice (one she must herself pound into a juju soap!) does she insist that he stop temporizing and show her the way home. This delay is probably no more justifiable than Odysseus' long stay with the goddess Calypso.[27] Simbi's trials and ordeals in Sinners' town, the town of the multi-coloured people, the land of poverty, and the Satyr's jungle are all laced together by her frequent expressions of regret that she has disobeyed her mother and foolishly sought the "poverty and the punishment" of life, together with the comments of her friends and enemies on her disobedience and folly.

Simbi's singing is involved in the motivations of the story to such an extent that it functions as a unifying device. Her singing in a town where singing is tabooed is the means by which she accidentally causes the death of her first master, and that accidental death motivates her being nailed up in a coffin and thrown into a river, so that she is fairly launched upon her adventures. Her singing, as we noted before, makes it possible for her to escape being sacrificed to the spirit of the king's head. And the Satyr, remembering her boasting about her singing, decides to construct the "illusive hall" as a "bait" for her.[28]

In this romance there are such anticipations of incidents as a reader would be more likely to expect in the work of sophisticated authors. Early in the book the badly disturbed Bako several times mentions her twin at home, a circumstance that she later uses to explain her own mad fits. The bush animals that fall into Simbi's game pit are carefully described as animals only in appearance, so that the reader is not surprised to see them later exercise more than animal powers. Simbi's abbreviation of the name Iromi (a water insect) to Iro in her first battle boast to the Satyr is rather portentously emphasized so that it will have the proper effect later when that abbreviation is responsible for the Satyr's death.[29]

The end of the romance is brisk, neat, and amusing, particularly Simbi and her friend Rali's being carried past Sinners' town in leather bags (the effects of the late Satyr) by two wayfarers smitten by the girls' beauty, and the bags being shuffled about by a series of robbers, until the girls are quite close to their home village.[30]

The Brave African Huntress is not so tightly organized as the previous novel, but it is by no means entirely episodic or haphazard in its organization. In the beginning there is a brisk exposition detailing the hunting prowess of Adebesi's father and the unsuccessful attempts of the father and many other hunters to kill all the wild animals and all the pigmies in the Jungle of the Pigmies and rescue Adebesi's four brothers "detained" there by the pigmies. This presents the situation requiring the quest, together with some interesting little matters like the father's gods that made fearful noises in the "half part of his house" that they occupied or the witches to whom he sacrificed, "the old and weary mothers" sleeping in "windowless and unventilated rooms." [31] Then follow—and quite naturally— Adebesi's resolve to undertake the quest when she hears a gossiping woman mention the loss of her brothers, whom she had never known, her repeated requests that her father let her go rescue her brothers (with his refusals), and her assiduous practice with various kinds of hunter's weapons. Once his permission is gained, the whole preparatory sequence is neatly rounded off with a moving scene in which Adebesi, in a kind of investiture ceremony, inherits the hunting profession of her father when her father invests her with the hunting gear, a ceremony complete with ceremonial eating and drinking and heart-felt prayers for the success of the Brave African Huntress starting out on her quest on Thursday, the Day of Creation.[32]

The huntress is quickly projected into her adventures: the second day of her quest the road she is following deadends into a "semi-jungle," the home of her first opponent. Only three adventures precede her engagements with the pigmy enemies: her encounter with Odara, the thrower of poisoned cudgels (so useful to Adebesi later) and his cruel "hooligan" followers; her freeing of Ibembe town from the predatory "semi-bird" (half human and half bird); and her comic trouble with the Ibembe king's hidden horns.[33] About a third of the way through the romance she starts to engage with the front line of the enemy: first she dispatches the fat, bullet-proof pigmy gatekeeper, one of Tutuola's amusing battle boasters ("All right, come and lay your head on this rock and let me cut it off."); then she shoots the pigmy guard on patrol, a surly brute called "obstacle [*sic*]," sporting a big "half fall goitre"; then she does in the many-horned, humming "super-animal," whose light-throwing eyes are useful to the heroine later. These conflicts are wonderfully varied brawls, full of happy inventions in mayhem and manslaughter that would make fortunes for TV writers, and there are sharp little graphic notations like "Within a few minutes we had scattered away all the dried leaves and refuses of that spot with our feet." [34]

When Adebesi is captured by the "huge stern pigmy" and he pushes her along toward the pigmies' town by his out-sized navel, she is entering upon her crucial struggles with her enemies, which begin with an ordeal in the pigmies' prison or "custody." The prison scenes move along briskly. The ragged, starving, spiritless prisoners are sketched in briefly but tellingly; a prisoner is beaten to death in front of the huntress; she has a miserable hard time lifting the heavy stones as she is required, and she is beaten by the cruel guards or "pesters" like the rest of the prisoners. But as soon as she is made a servant in the prison office she plants the gunpowder that will destroy the prison, and quickly offends the chief keeper enough for him to condemn her to death and give her the occasion to escape from the prison by playing dead. So she is in a position to fire the pigmy town, destroy the prison (freeing the prisoners), and disperse those pigmies she does not manage to shoot down—by the light of her helmet made from the skull of "the animal that died but his eyes are still alive." [35] The "custody" sequence has some of the best humorous scenes of the romance: the blind pigmy king who shakes hands with the wrong person; Adebesi and the "deputy keeper" standing at attention for two hours while the "chief keeper" drinks his liquor and ignores them; Adebesi, as prison office servant, caught drinking the "chief keeper's" liquor. [36]

After the huntress' devastating attack on the pigmy stronghold, some of the episodes are dubiously relevant. Her escape from the pigmy town where she has been trapped by a rock slide is perhaps admissible, though the means—a lassoed, reluctant gorilla hauling her up through a tree fallen over the cliff—is not altogether credible. Certain episodes would seem to be clearly superfluous: the wild episode at the river in which the "snake of snakes" butts Adebesi into the drink and she takes a ride piggyback on a hippo; the delightful and humorous story of Adebesi's very comfortable and flattering life as Queen of the Bachelors' town until she looks into the forbidden room; her battle with the "snake of snakes" and her stay with the kind old man tormented by the trickster and robber Ajantala.[37] These episodes toward the end of the romance, on the other hand, would be entirely relevant: the huntress' first brush with a party of surviving pigmies; her capture and torture by such a party of pigmies, and her subsequent escape; her shooting the surviving pigmies in their second town; her furious battle with the last and most dangerous pigmy; her meeting with her four brothers and other hometown men; their Robinson Crusoe style preparations for going home; the canoe trip down the river to the home town; and their welcome home, with the "great merriment" to celebrate their homecoming.[38] The winding up of the romance is notably swift and cheerful: the happy men and the Brave African Huntress go paddling down river toward home singing their ice cream song.[39]

The organizing devices in this romance are as conspicuous as in the previous romance, though the same devices are not used. Especially conspicuous are the time signals, like "about eleven o'clock," "when the dove gave the sign of eight o'clock," "for about three weeks," and "about six months." There are enough of these to make the reader think he could plot an accurate time-chart of the incidents —probably an illusion.[40] Anticipations alert the reader to coming events regarding the "super-animal," "the pigmy town," and the boa constrictor or "snake of snakes." [41] Another organizing device, one that is not entirely successful, is the cluster of epigraphs at the head of most of the chapters and within a few of the chapters; these seem designed to link together the materials within chapters; they are echoed within the chapter over which they appear. Often, however, the connection between the epigraph and the text is rather tenuous, entailing considerable hunting and calculation on the part of the reader. Sometimes statements or phrases within the epigraph have a proverbial ring to them, as "The rain does not know the honorable person apart. But the rain soaks anybody who comes out when it is raining." Sometimes the proverbial allusion is cryptic, as in the reference to the "kakaki trumpet" blown only for a king: "The thief who steals bugle. Where is he going to blow it? In the world of the white men or the Heaven?" [42] Another organizing device, one that appears more rarely than in the earlier romances, is that hold-over from the oral method, the little summary, as "And that was how I came out from the Bachelors' town."

As in the previous romance the heroine sticks religiously to the business of her quest. She does get lost in the bush several times, but that is understandable and forgivable. Her getting lost in the vicinity of Bachelors' town may partly justify the apparently irrelevant episode associated with that locale. And it must be admitted that her stay at Ibembe town and with the kind old man have reasons assigned to justify them: her "barbing" the king with his secret horns in gratitude for the gunpowder and shot he has given her, and her desperate need for rest after some very strenuous exertions. In her splendor and her flattered ease as Queen among the bachelors she momentarily loses her desire to go on with the quest or to go home, but who can blame her, and besides, at least one home-forgetting episode seems to be part of the *Odyssey* tradition.[43]

Feather Woman of the Jungle is also, comparatively speaking, tightly organized. In this work a number of tales are gathered in a framework: a new chief relates to his villagers six of his journeys or fortune-hunting expeditions in ten "entertainments" or story telling sessions on successive moonlight nights during the dry season. The first journey, involving the Feather Woman and her bird cohorts and her images (all enchanted persons) takes two entertainments; the fifth journey, detailing the narrator's trials and triumphs in the town of the Goddess of Diamonds and his elopement with the Goddess' daughter Sela, has a sequel in a following entertainment, the vivid account of the kidnapping of Sela amid earthquake, storm, fire, and fighting with two very strange warriors of the Goddess. The sixth journey, the search for the underground town full of treasures, takes up the last three entertainments. (Before the very short chapter laying in the setting for the story telling sessions, Tutuola provides a curious little "Biography of my Town in Brief," giving a brief account of the Egba people's founding of Abeokuta and explanations on "type of houses built," "daily tasks," "tribal marks," "plays and amusements," "means of communications," and "believes." Apparently intended as a kind of cultural introduction to the Egba Yorubas for Western readers, this note is not necessary for understanding the following stories, and does not fit the total design of the work. Some of the proverbial wisdom delivered by the narrator in the entertainments of the third night and the fifth night seem similarly irrelevant.)

Only three of the tales seem entirely independent of the others: the tale of the rescue and restoration of the King of the Bush of Quietness who has been so deceived, abused, and tormented by his unfaithful queen (third night); the tale of the relief of the town of starving persons by the magic food box procured from the underwater people (fifth night); and the tale of the chief's tribulations suffered among the savage people, especially at the hands of the ogress called a "dangerous night creature" and the "senior chief" of the savage people, who ride him horseback in his cave.

Most of the tales have links with tales in other entertainments. In the second entertainment Ashabi's faithful career as a "dump" (dumb) queen greatly tempted to speak relieves her brothers from their transformation into images, which they undergo in the first entertainment. The spouse that the narrator elopes with in the sixth entertainment is kidnapped from him in the seventh entertainment. In the eighth entertainment the tourist-style sight-seeing in Ife (the holy city of the Yorubas) and Ede—"The Foot Marks of the First White Men who had travelled from Heaven to the World . . . the Wells from which the sun and moon are rising into the Sky . . . the God of Thunder and his Wife"—is insisted upon by the "porter" who must show them the entrance to the underground, where the wayfarers will find the "town of wealths," and have the adventures described in the entertainment of the ninth night. This entertainment deals mostly with the wayfarers' conflict with the Hairy Giant and Giantess that the "porter" had warned them about in the previous entertainment. The last entertainment, besides the struggle with the madman with his flaming pot, details the successful larceny in the "town of wealth" (the goal of this last journey), the escape from the town in a canoe, the storm at sea, the canoe wreck on the beach near the town of the Goddess of Diamonds, the reunion of the narrator with his wife Sela (adventures echoing events in the sixth and seventh entertainments), and the successful removal of diamonds to repair the complete loss of assets when the narrator's apartment building burned in the raid of the Goddess' men (seventh entertainment).

The character of the narrator, who is the main character in all the tales, also unifies the series. He is the older brother of the two boys and the girl going on the first journey. He is alone in the second, fourth, and fifth journeys. He is accompanied only by his trusty hunting dogs in the third journey. In the sixth journey he leads six companions.

Most of the journeys have the same motivation, the pursuit of wealth. True, the narrator undertakes his second journey in order to have as many "difficulties" as the "old people," and he wins wealth though that was not his purpose: the prince who marries his sister gives him many costly presents which he sells for profit. Even when the narrator has a financial competence, he goes out on another journey: the fourth; he needs wealth for a rainy day, as it were, for "We did not know of tomorrow." [44] After the narrator has invested his savings in a "storey" or apartment house and it is burned down with all his other assets, he has to start all over again in his pursuit of wealth. He starts out for the underground town which has treasures that the inhabitants do not prize (!), and of course he succeeds in getting booty from this town and—unexpectedly—from the city of the Goddess of Diamonds.

Numerous workmanlike transitions between the tales, usually with time indications, fasten the tales together in their framework, as "So tomorrow I shall continue to tell you the adventure of my third journey," "After a few days that I had returned from second journey," "But I continued my fifth journey after one year that I had returned from the town of famine," and "So in the morning that I completed one year that I had brought Sela to the village . . . ." [45] There are a few anticipations of coming events and a few of the summarizing tags described above. On two occasions the narrator briefly relates his recent adventures to a character in a tale. Once the narrator dreams of a character encountered in a previous journey. [46]

The unifying effect of the framework is strengthened by several kinds of repetition. At each gathering to hear the evening's entertainment, the villagers enjoy the Nigerian amenities, both before and after the story-telling. So before and after each tale occurs the repetitive formula: *palm-wine drinking, dancing and singing.* Sometimes one or more of the activities of this fictional refrain is omitted. Sometimes the activity of *drumming* is added. [47] The formula does not appear at the end of the eighth night's entertainment. The narrator's pipe is repeatedly mentioned in the beginning of the third, sixth, seventh, and eighth entertainments, and the easy chair he sits in as he tells his stories in the first, third, sixth, seventh, and eighth entertainments. Almost all of the entertainments show another repetitive formula: *my gun, my hunting bag and my matchet,* with occasional omission of one of the items, or other variations, paralleling the character of the narrator as a constant throughout the series of tales. [48]

VI *Novel or Quest Romance?*

Most reviewers of Tutuola's books have taken for granted that they are meant to be novels, and this misconception has made for a good deal of critical clumsiness in judgment and some unfairness.

If we suppose that the novel proper is a piece of prose fiction that has realistic characters, that deals with man in social relations, usually in a more or less contemporary setting, then surely the Tutuola works are something else again and are not fairly judged as novels.[49]

Gerald Moore notices this mistake in placing Tutuola's fiction and reorients us by saying that Tutuola's "affinities are with Bunyan, Dante and Blake rather than with the Western novel." He calls Tutuola a "visionary" and his books "prose epics rather than novels." But though the names of Bunyan, Dante, and Blake usefully highlight the mythopoeic, non-realistic quality of Tutuola's works, only Bunyan is a fiction writer, and Moore does not pursue the very significant parallels between Bunyan and Tutuola beyond saying that neither had much formal education and both "seize upon the images of popular imagination and use them for their own purposes." The term "visionary" is somewhat vague for literary analysis, and "prose epic" is easily confused with Fielding's "comic epic in prose." [50]

A really accurate genre-name for Tutuola's works would be "naive romances"; "naive" to distinguish them from the more sophisticated romances of William Morris or perhaps Hawthorne. The romance genre has been brilliantly distinguished and analyzed by Northrop Frye in his *Anatomy of Criticism*. Frye's placing of the "romance mode of fiction" by the degree of the "hero's power of action" seems exactly pertinent to Tutuola's ghost novels:

If superior in *degree* to other men and to his environment, the hero is the typical hero of *romance*, whose actions are marvelous but who is himself identified as a human being. The hero of romance moves in a world in which the ordinary laws of nature are slightly suspended; prodigies of courage and endurance, unnatural to us, are natural to him, and enchanted weapons, talking animals, terrifying ogres and witches, and talismans of miraculous power violate no rule of probability once the postulates of romance have been established. Here we have moved from myth, properly so called (in which the hero has powers superior in kind, is a divine being), into legend, folk tale, märchen, and their literary affiliates and derivatives.

If the reader objects that Tutuola's heroes are in fact godlike in their powers, we might reply that Frye's modes of fiction shade off into each other and that Frye explicitly notes that romances sometimes approach the myth: "The enemy may be an ordinary human being

[Dogo, the slaver in *Simbi,* for instance], but the nearer the romance to myth, the more attributes of divinity will cling to the hero and the more the enemy will take on demonic mythical quialities." [51] Drinkard refers to himself with dubious modesty as "Father of Gods," and he claims he "can do everything in this world."

Frye indicates the structural principle organizing the incidents in a romance as the Quest:

The complete form of the romance is clearly the successful quest, and such a completed form has three main stages: the stage of the perilous journey and the preliminary adventures, the crucial struggle, usually some kind of battle in which either the hero or his foe, or both, must die; and the exultation of the hero. [52]

Tutuola's romances are rather more episodic than Frye's scheme suggests; that is, the episodes are often interchangeable in position —as in such extended Yoruba tales as the stories about Tinringin or about the Tortoise in the Itayemi-Gurrey Penguin collection of West African folk tales. [53]

Drinkard's quest is of course his search for his dead palm-wine tapster in Deads' Town (reminding us of other mythological and literary figures going on that particular journey—Orpheus, Hercules, Theseus, Odysseus, Aeneas, and Dante). In *The Palm-Wine Drinkard* it is not easy to distinguish Frye's "crucial struggle" from the "minor adventures"; the shooting of the red fish and the red bird which have been getting annual human sacrifices is important but perhaps no more crucial than nearly being executed through the wiles of the "prince-killer," which also occurs just before the arrival at Deads' Town. And the fight with the red creatures is no more exciting than a number of other fights, trials, and experiences, like Drinkard's capturing Death in a net, his rescuing Drinkard's wife from the Skull and his family, the troubles with the monstrous, quick-growing, ravenous, bullying baby born out of Drinkard's wife's left thumb, the tortures (being beaten, whipped, stoned, buried to the chin, their heads scraped with pieces of a broken bottle, being smeared with excrement) at the hands of the mad and cruel eccentrics of Unreturnable-Heaven's town, the pleasant stay at Faithful-Mother's resort-hotel-cum-hospital, the vicious dead babies assaulting Drinkard and his wife on the way home from Deads' Town, their being swallowed by Hungry Creature and Drinkard's shooting him from inside his stomach and cutting a way out with the cutlass, or their escaping from the mountain-creatures by Drinkard's changing them into a stone and throwing it along the road and over the river. Drinkard's exultation would be his feeding his town in a famine with the magic egg given him by the dead tapster friend (like Orpheus he could not bring the dead back), and after his punishing the crowd for its misbehavior, bringing the famine to an end by the sacrifice to heaven.[54]

My Life in the Bush of Ghosts describes the narrator's twenty-four years of wandering on his way home through a jungle where frightful spirits roam. The wanderer engages in a kind of quest in reverse, or West African Odyssey. Or perhaps it could be called a purgatory or an initiation into the "Meaning of 'Bad' and 'Good'" imposed on him. Separated from his brother in a slave raid and blundering into the Bush of Ghosts, he has a series of extraordinary experiences, most of them terrifying; he is, among other things, "bagged" by a malodorous Smelling-Ghost, transformed into a cow, "corked" in a hollow log and used as a music box, baptized with fire and hot water in Rev. Devil's church, worshipped as a big-headed, long-necked god in a pitcher, wrapped up in a spider web, buried alive, "flogged with fire" by the monumental flash-eyed mother, almost "barbed" with scissors of fire, and decapitated in a ghost war and his head replaced by a ghost's head. There is no crucial struggle. The quarrel with his second wife, Super Lady, and his enjoyable sojourn with his dead cousin, the Methodist bishop, precede his return, when he is urged by the fortune-teller's magnetic missive and the home scenes provided by the Television-handed Ghostess.[55] The exultation would be the joyful reunion with his brother and his mother, after he has sung the song by which his brother recognizes him. On recognizing him, his brother shouts with gladness, has his "orderlies" wash him and dress him in costly clothes "as a king," and has his wives serve him food and drink.

The quest described in *Simbi and the Satyr of the Dark Jungle* (one involving Simbi's disobedience to her mother) is Simbi's search for the "poverties and punishments of life," which she finds in full measure, at least the "punishments," for she is enslaved, beaten by other slaves, nailed in a coffin and dumped in a river, almost sacrificed to the spirit of a king's head (a curious religious notion of the Yorubas), assaulted by a crazed companion, almost executed for a theft, trapped in a hollow tree, almost eaten by a boa constrictor, dive-bombed by a phoenix bird, welded to a rock and beaten "greedily" by the satyr and his followers. (It is hard to think of these as "minor" adventures.) The crucial struggle is Simbi's second battle with the Satyr, in which she changes herself into a water insect, crawls up into the Satyr's nose, and stings him to death, while his followers laugh at his agonized movements "with the intention that he was simply playing." The exultation is clearly defined; Simbi and her friend are carried home in bags by the two wayfarers who have "lost all their senses in respect of the beauty of the two ladies," Simbi cudgels the slaver Dogo into a promise to stop kidnapping the villagers, her happy mother welcomes her home by killing "all kinds of domestic animals for the merriments," and Simbi is reconciled to her mother and goes about from house to house in the village telling the girls they should obey their mothers, lest they suffer as she has suffered for disobeying her mother.[56]

The quest in *The Brave African Huntress* is a rescue mission. Adebesi, daughter of a great hunter and, contrary to custom, the inheritor of his traditional profession, sets out to find her four hunter brothers who have been killed or "detained" by the hostile pigmies in their jungle; besides rescuing her brothers she means to "kill or drive the whole pigmies away from that jungle" and to kill all the dangerous wild animals. After she encounters an ogre with a poisoned cudgel, a man-eating bird, a riot over a royal scandal, a big-headed pigmy gatekeeper with varicose veins, the pigmy guard called an "obstacle," the "animal that died but his eyes still alive," the huge stern pigmy, and the keepers and "pesters" of a pigmy prison, the crucial struggle comes. The huntress escapes from the "custody" and destroys the pigmy town by fire and gunpowder charges, shooting down the bewildered pigmies as they run about.

The exultation is about what we expect: Adebesi finds her four brothers among four hundred hunters escaped from the pigmy town. Adebesi and the hunters, like Robinson Crusoes, carve "mighty trees" into canoes for a trip down river to the home village; they paddle down the river, singing the chocolate and ice cream song, and are of course welcomed with "merriments." Adebesi sells the minerals she has found in the Jungle of the Pigmies and becomes a rich woman. But between the destruction of the pigmy town and the happy return home there is a sort of interlude of incidents, exultant and otherwise. Pulled out of the destroyed pigmy town by a gorilla, she is magically transferred to a Bachelors' town, where she becomes a pampered queen until she looks into the forbidden room. Then she stays with an old man who is tormented by a bullying trickster. She is about to be killed by a party of pigmies but escapes.

She is surrounded by a large number of snakes and kills "the whole of them," by pounding them with a cutlass and a poisonous cudgel. Then she mops up the remainder of the pigmies, shooting them in the light of the beams from the reflecting eyes of the "super-animal." [57]

The quest in *Feather Woman of the Jungle* is a search for money to relieve the poverty and pay the debts of the narrator's father and mother. The new chief of a village relates to his people six of his journeys or adventures in his search for wealth. The chief's "minor adventures" are sufficiently exciting and bizarre. The Feather Woman, who changes offenders into birds and "images," changes the chief into an image (with human feelings) and flogs him regularly every morning. He straightens out the affairs of the king in the Bush of Quietness, whose unfaithful wife has transformed his lower body to snake form and beats him every midnight. He is captured by the "savage people" when their king's bellowing voice shakes the chief out of a tree; their "senior chief" rides him like a horse. He relieves a famine in a town by going down under water to the Queen of the River, who gives him a magic food box. From the Goddess of Diamonds' town on the mountain top, he runs off with the Goddess' daughter, Sela, and a quantity of diamonds, but the Goddess sends some men to his village who come like a combination earthquake and hurricane and take the girl back. He sees some marvelous sights in Ife (the sacred city of the Yorubas) and visits the thunder god in Ede. The crucial struggle would be their adventure in the underground "town of wealths," where he and his friends have a long-drawn-out fight with a Hairy Giant and Giantess, who try to roast them in a fire, and finally they manage to push the giant pair over a cliff into a river. In this underground area four of their men are killed by a "terrible mad man." Trying to steal away from the town with two gold blocks, they are captured, thrown in prison and beaten badly. But they escape and outdistance their pursuers in a canoe, which is wrecked at the base of the mountain on which stands the town of the Goddess of Diamonds. The exultation comes when with his last remaining friend he climbs the mountain and meets Sela, with whom he runs off again, together with "plenty of the diamond blocks." A rich man, his mission accomplished, after his adventures the chief and his wife "are living comfortably." [58]

VII *The Romances and Campbell's Heroic Monomyth*

In the chapter on Tutuola in his *Seven African Writers,* Gerald

Moore explains the structures of the romances by tracing in them the motifs of "one variant or another of the cycle of the heroic mono-myth, Departure—Initiation—Return, as analyzed by Joseph Camp-bell in *The Hero of a Thousand Faces*." In *The Palm-Wine Drinkard* the variant form is the

deliberate, limited Quest, Drinkard's quest for his dead palm-wine tapster and the ordeals and revelations he experiences in that quest. Drinkard's binding and delivering of Death is a clear indication that his adventure is "not merely an adventure into the eternal African bush, but equally a journey into the racial imagination, into the subconscious, into that Spirit World that everywhere co-exists and even overlaps with the world of waking reality."

Familiar figures of the monomyth appear: taskmasters who demand certain labors as a price for directions for finding the dead tapster, the loyal female companion in the person of his wife (like Dante's Beatrice and Theseus' Ariadne), and the devouring monster (the red fish) levying an annual human sacrifice on a community. Per-haps Drinkard has fewer magic helpers than European folk heroes because he has his very powerful juju. The half-bodied baby is very like the Tom Thumb of European folklore. The vacation with Faithful-Mother seems to Moore an example of what Campbell calls "Meeting with the Mother Goddess," and her White Tree, the usual tree symbol for the World Navel (as Igdrasil, the Bo Tree, the Tree of Knowledge in Eden). Drinkard and his wife's uncomfortable stay inside the hungry-creature reminds Moore of the familiar motif of the Whale's Belly.

Although Drinkard cannot bring back his tapster, he experiences an important initiation: he learns from the tapster the true meaning of life and death, and he receives from his friend a gift of a magic egg which will do whatever he wishes it to do. Drinkard is trans-formed; he has "undergone his 'rite of passage.'" The river Drinkard and his wife cross over by magical means on their way home, hotly pursued by the mountain creatures, is for Moore the mythical Return Threshold, which pursuers can never cross. As usual with a returning "boon-bearing hero," Moore notes, Drinkard finds his community in "anarchy and distress"; the town is suffering from a famine. First he tries to save the town by producing food with his magic egg, but when human greed frustrates him, he brings the famine to an end by reconciling Heaven and Earth, whose quarrel is causing the famine, sending a slave to Heaven with a gift to acknowledge Heaven's seniority (according to Moore, recognizing the supremacy of the male Sky God, over the female Earth Goddess, protectress of matriarchy). As Moore interprets the hero's Quest, Drinkard's new understanding, won in his quest, makes it possible for him to save his people by such cosmic peacemaking.[59]

By the same token, *My Life in the Bush of Ghosts,* Moore thinks, is a kind of extended initiation or "rite of passage." At the beginning of the story the narrator is a young boy in a "state of innocence," just starting to know the "bad," since he suffers from the jealousy of his father's wives, but not yet knowing the meaning of "good." His many, mostly fearful, experiences in the Bush of Ghosts (non-human spirits) presumably give him a full knowledge of good and evil; he is a kind of West African Adam.[60]

Moore sees *Simbi and the Satyr of the Dark Jungle* as the account of the self-imposed ordeals of a well-off young lady who believes that her "advantages must ultimately be paid for by comparable abasement and suffering," because "in myth it is seen that *Man himself,* by heroic action or sacrifice, must renew the energy of the world and keep it in equipoise." Moore notes that Simbi starts her journey at the "place where three paths meet"—a common point of departure for mythical journeys. On one occasion she is saved from her enemy the Satyr by the magical helper, common in the mythical quest.[61]

The reader sympathetic to Campbell's approach, which makes a sort of universal philosophy-religion out of the myths of the world, might care to extend Moore's brilliant analysis on these monomyth lines. Even if we are not persuaded by the analysis, we must admit that the folk motifs used by Tutuola are very widespread, whether by diffusion or independent invention. We need only to browse through Stith Thompson's massive *Motif-Index of Folk-Literature* which contains many analogues to Tutuolan incidents, even the most fanciful, to be reminded how folk literatures assert our common humanity.[62]

A random sampling of the geographical distribution of parallels, more or less close, for some Tutuolan motifs shows how widespread such motifs are (numbers give locations in the *Index*): Drinkard's quick-growing, precocious child—Greece, Iceland, Ireland, India (T585); Drinkard's changing himself to a canoe—Hawaii (D255.1); Drinkard's cutting his way out of the hungry-creature's stomach— Cameroon, Basutoland, Cook Islands, Eastern Brazil, Marquesas

(F912.1); Drinkard's changing himself into a pebble to escape the pursuing "mountain creatures"—Bechuanaland, Northern Rhodesia, Zululand (D671.0.7); the wanderer in the Bush of Ghosts' being changed into a cow—Greece, Iceland, India (D133.1); Simbi's changing herself into an insect and flying into the Satyr's nostrils and stinging him to death—Iceland, South America (F531.1.8.5; K952.2).[63]

A common criticism of Tutuola's romances, even from critics generally sympathetic, is that they all become tedious at last, that they "are a little too much of the same repeated," as Robie Macauley puts it.[64] Probably what these critics have in mind is that, over and over, Tutuola has his heroes and heroines engage in furious physical conflicts with ogres. For instance, after three ogre-filled romances, Tutuola has the Brave African Huntress of the fourth romance tangle with six ogres or ogreish pigmies before she reaches the town of the pigmies, that is, in the space of seventy-nine pages. And though there is considerable variety in the appearance and manners of at least the major monsters, such as the flash-eyed mother, Smelling-Ghost, and Feather Woman, there is also a certain sameness about many of them and about the encounters with them.

Another cause of tedium which some of the critics may be responding to is the fact that the reader of a Tutuola romance does not always get a sense of narrative progression, a firm notion of how an episode contributes to the quest or initiation of the romance— Drinkard's search for his tapster in the underworld, the wanderer's enforced initiation into mature understanding in the Bush of Ghosts, Simbi's quest for a knowledge of "the poverties" and "the punishments of life," the huntress' rescue of her brothers from the cruel pigmies, and the various commercial quests of the narrator's "entertainments." It is as though the reader is in one of those nightmares in which the same terrible thing or some version of it is happening over and over and over. It surely is not tedious in the dreams, but it *is* somewhat in Tutuola's romances, though this writer believes that the tedium complained of is much exaggerated by the critics.

VIII *A Dramatization*

In connection with the episodic quality of Tutuola's works, the structure of the stage version of *The Palm-Wine Drinkard* forms an interesting contrast with that of the original romance. Kola Ogunmola's highly successful Yoruba-language stage version of *The Palm-Wine Drinkard*, based on Tutuola's own unpublished English dramatic version, is less crowded and more tightly organized than most of the romances. Instead of the more than twenty episodes of *The Palm-Wine Drinkard* (of one hundred twenty-five pages), the play has only eight episodes: Drinkard's drinking party with his friends, including a "praise song" for palm-wine and a riddle game (both added); his encounter with the Night Spirit; his dealings with the two white gods and his fetching of Death for them; Drinkard's wife's misadventure with the Complete Gentleman (the skull) and Drinkard's rescuing of her; the meeting with the Cruel King and the Sickness Seller; the sojourn with Faithful-Mother and Drinkard's marriage at her home; the visit with the dead tapster in Deads' Town; and Drinkard's changing water into wine with the magic egg brought from Deads' Town.

Other modifications have been made in the interest of dramatic structure. The Night Spirit, not found in *The Palm-Wine Drinkard* but rather like the "dangerous night creature" of *Feather Woman of the Jungle,* has a clear function in the play, to provide Drinkard with a charm to see him safely through his perilous journey. The white gods who set Drinkard his task of fetching Death seem to merge four figures in *The Palm-Wine Drinkard:* the old man and his wife who are gods setting this task in the original romance (no color mentioned), the "white pillar" god, and the kneeling female figure who is "cream-coloured," the latter two mentioned later. The episode with the Cruel King and the Sickness Seller serves as a climax among the ordeals in the play; the king seems to be based on the king in the Sinners' town in *Simbi,* and the Sickness Seller is new in the Tutuola canon but has the Tutuola touch (and also the Yoruba folk tale touch). The stay with Faithful-Mother ties up a loose thread: it gives an occasion for Drinkard's marriage with the lady he has rescued, a detail neglected in the romance. The egg's changing water into wine, instead of making food, as in the romance, emphasizes the palm-wine theme and recalls the bacchanalian opening of the play. The fact that all of the incidents after the palm-wine party are *dreamed* by the wine-befuddled Drinkard rationalizes, as it were, whatever disconnectedness remains.[65] It would be interesting to know how Tutuola's prolific multiplicity came to be curbed. Did the translator and producer Ugunmola cut and revise, or did Tutuola himself, with the advice of Professor Collis of the University of Ibadan, "neaten" the exuberant plenty?

CHAPTER 3

The Folklore Basis of the Romances

I Nigerian Reactions to Tutuola's Work

MOST West African objections to Tutuola's work have had to
do with its basis in traditional Yoruba folklore. West Africans
complained of the "commonplace" character of the stories in his
novels; they had heard such stories from their grandmothers, they
said. Some went so far as to suggest plagiarism from a printed collection of folk tales.[1] Such objections were understandable, as we
shall see, but they were misguided.

Though entirely correct about the folklore content of the novels
and about Tutuola's adapting folk tales they had heard from their
grandmothers, these critics were completely wrong in complaining
about commonplaceness and plagiarism. Their complaints were
founded on an erroneous but widespread misconception of literary
originality that equates it with novelty of action, theme, setting, and
so on. Tutuola does new things with the traditional tales, handles
them creatively. The brilliant Yoruba folk tales are a common pos-
session of the Yoruba people, folk property, not copyrighted private
property, and so a gifted individual artist like Tutuola has every
right to adapt them, elaborate them, sophisticate them, do with them
what he will, and can. No matter how familiar they might be to a
Nigerian, the Yoruba folk tales ought never to be considered commonplace, any more than the myths of Oedipus, of Prometheus, or
of the Fall of Man. And as for plagiarism, we might simply say that
Tutuola came by his folk tales in exactly the same way that every
traditional narrator does; in a narrator of the oral literature we must
not expect the kind of originality that we do in ordinary authors in
written literature: the originality comes in the treatment of the
familiar stories. After he had written *My Life in the Bush of Ghosts*
he felt written out: he returned to Abeokuta, not to consult the public
library there (if there is one), but to listen to the old people telling
Yoruba tales.[2]

Fortunately, Nigerians are becoming increasingly respectful toward their traditional customs, religious beliefs, and folk literature, and probably the folklore basis of Tutuola's work will be considered more sensibly in the future. Anyone at all familiar with Yoruba folk tales will attest to their high value and their worth as a contribution to world culture. Their shrewd and realistic appraisal of human nature, their sharp social realism, their astonishing fancy, their wonderful unrestrained humor and high spirits, their level-headed celebration of such precious human virtues as prudence, good management, common sense, good-natured kindness, steady loyalty, and courage ought to be admired by readers the world over in some such sprightly, lively form as Tutuola's folk novels; they ought not to be buried in learned journals and specialized books. Tutuola must have some sort of sense that he is bringing the riches of his oral tradition to the world; his updating, Westernizing, adapting of these tales suggests that he knows what he is doing. By now, probably, most educated Nigerians have gotten over the shock of Tutuola's crudity and backwardness, and understand that since something has to be done with the oral tradition, his use of it is in many ways quite admirable. But before we go into the question of the advisability of using Nigerian folk tales as a basis of Nigerian fiction, we should take a closer look at just what happens when Tutuola adapts a folk tale.

II *How Tutuola Uses Folk Tales*

An examination of African folk tale collections, especially those collecting Yoruba tales, like the Yoruba section of Phebean Itayemi and P. Gurrey's *Folk Tales and Fables,* M. I. Ogumefu's *Yoruba Legends,* and Barbara and Warren Walker's *Nigerian Tales,* will uncover a score or more parallels and possible sources for incidents in Tutuola's novels, including some of the most striking, and those which would seem most likely to be original with Tutuola. At the same time, such an examination will also make abundantly clear how freely Tutuola adapts his folk material for his own purposes. We will consider a few of these parallels, noting how widely distributed some of Tutuola's motifs are.

One of Tutuola's best episodes, in *The Palm-Wine Drinkard*—the story of the willful beauty eloping with a handsome stranger, who on the way to his home gives back the *rented* parts of his body and his members until he is a skull—appears in a number of versions in the various collections. In the Ogumefu version he has borrowed, not rented, his body parts, and the lady escapes him simply because he cannot pursue her without legs. In the version in Elphinstone Dayrell's *Folk Stories of Southern Nigeria,* the skull's parts are borrowed, and the lady is blown home by a wind called up by her anxious mother. In a version in Alta Jablow's *Yes and No: The Intimate Folklore of Africa,* the skull's parts are borrowed; the disobedient daughter is befriended by her mother-in-law, to whom she has been very helpful, and it is the mother-in-law who arranges for the homecoming wind. Besides the *renting* of the skull's body, Tutuola has contributed a great deal of elaboration on the willful beauty's fascination with the handsome stranger and that stranger's extraordinary beauty (he was so handsome that if he was in a town to be bombed, "bombers would not throw bomb on his presence, or if they did throw it, the bomb itself would not explode . . . ."), Drinkard's careful "investigation to the skull's family's house," the conditions of the lady's imprisonment (in a cave, sitting on a frog, with an alarm-sounding cowrie around her neck, and enchanted into dumbness), the exciting rescue with its transformations and Drinkard flying through the air with her, the subsequent removal of the noisy cowrie from the lady's neck, and the cure of her dumbness and lack of appetite.[3]

Child-Wiser-than-His Father in the Itayemi-Gurrey collection is rather like Drinkard's monstrous child, being a quick grower and quick talker and a pest to his parents, though he is born from his mother's big toe, not her thumb, like Drinkard's monstrous child. Child-Wiser-than-His Father is more of a trickster than Drinkard's child, who is a bullying brawler eating and drinking a family out of house and home and tormenting a whole village with his "havocs and bad character." Obviously Drinkard's child cannot kill his own father and make his mother eat the father's liver, as Child-Wiser-than-His-Father does, for Drinkard must tell the story. Another important difference is that Drinkard's monstrous child, when he is burned to death by his father, is resurrected as "half-baby," with the "lower voice like a telephone" and in this form makes his parents carry him about and feed him continually without eating or sleeping themselves, until he finally is lured off their backs, as it were, by the celebrations of Drum, Song, and Dance.[4]

Drinkard's magic egg, producing food inexhaustibly for a famine-stricken multitude, and when "regummed" producing whips to whip an unruly and ungrateful crowd, is like a great number of magical food producers and punishers of disagreeable persons in African folk tales, and indeed in other folk literatures. In a story in the Itayemi-Gurrey collection the Yoruba folk hero Tortoise has a magic ladle that ladles out food to a crowd and whips them in a locked compound when they deserve it. In a story in Dayrell's collection, a king's magic drum, when certain taboos are broken, produces men whipping the expectant crowd. In a version recorded by Ogumefu, Tortoise discovers a small "chop tree" and a large whip tree. His wife and relations are destroyed by the whip tree, and many townsmen investigating their disappearance are badly beaten. Among Tutuola's contributions to this motif are his graphic descriptions of the clamoring, unruly crowd (including a number of kings and their attendants) and its precipitate flight from the whips, leaving behind children and old persons, and the ending of the famine by a sacrifice of fowls, colas, and palm oil carried to heaven by a slave.[5]

W. H. Barker and Cecilia Sinclair have recorded a story about a magic food producer: a kind old woman in an underground village helps Kweku Tsin, son of the Ashanti trickster hero Anansi the Spider, to procure a magic drum that feeds his village during a famine; his father, jealous of his son's prestige, tries to get such a drum, but he rudely refuses to follow the old woman's directions, gets a drum that says "dong-dong" rather than "ding-ding," and the drum produces not food, but beasts and serpents.[6]

One of the two legal cases Drinkard is asked to judge in the "mixed town" is rather like a story recorded by Jablow (from the BaKongo!) about a man who dies and whose wives revive him and then quarrel over who should take most credit for doing so: one had dreamed where the husband's body was, one had guided the other wives to the spot, and the other had brought him back to life with certain herbs. The three wives in Tutuola's version are with him when he dies: one dies for him right there and then, one goes and gets a wizard who brings him back to life, and the other watches his body to protect it from wild animals while the wizard is being brought. For a reward the wizard asks for one of the wives, but each seems to have a good claim not to be given up. Drinkard, required to decide who shall be given to the wizard, postpones the trial for a year and leaves town.[7]

Itayemi and Gurrey include a tale about two brothers separated by a slave raid and reunited by the younger brother's singing a sad song familiar to his brother—precisely the framework story of *My Life in the Bush of Ghosts*. Tutuola, besides using the story to frame his other incidents, has added a wife, jealous of the brothers and their mother, who abandons them in the slave raid. He makes the older brother cruel to his slaves, among whom the younger brother finds himself at the end of the novel, and so the reunion of the brothers is more exciting and pathetic than in the Itayemi-Gurrey version.[8]

One of Tutuola's best character creations is Super Lady, she of the "lofty smiling face" fresh as "angel's face" and of the solemn voice, the lady anachronistically possessing a Western-style house which is fit, we would suppose, for a Nigerian senior service man (besides the usual rooms it has a dressing room). Super Lady is probably a wonderful adaptation of a heroine in a Yoruba demon lover tale. As recorded by Barbara and Warren Walker, the tale concerns a hunter who marries a deer woman; she picks up her deer skin (from the attic!) and leaves him because his human wife has taunted her about her animal origin. Tutuola's wanderer first sees Super Lady as an antelope, and she has impressive powers of self-transformation. Her mother is a witch and her father a wizard, both being prominent in professional witching activities, but she herself is harmless. She and the wanderer quarrel over the upbringing of their child, who is half-ghost and half-human in his behavior, and she drives her husband out of town.[9]

Itayemi and Gurrey also provide a parallel to the episode in which the wanderer in the Bush of Ghosts molds an arm of mud for the one-armed wife of the king who is about to be discovered by the kingmakers and prominent ghosts of the town in the crime of marrying an "amputy." In the Itayemi-Gurrey version, the wife has no teeth; she gets a new set on her mother's grave, and her accusers' teeth all fall out. In Tutuola's version he builds up the dramatic values of the inspection very well: the king's wives are to pound corn before the town's big-wigs. The jealous accusing wives are all killed rather than disabled; there is a rule against telling lies against the king. The king welshes on his promise to tell the wanderer the way home; he wants the wanderer to stay in his town fifteen more years. The wanderer simply ducks out.[10]

One of Simbi's hairbreadth escapes looks rather like a tale from Ghana recorded by Barker and Sinclair in which a hunter saves a leopard, a serpent, a rat, and a man from a pit. In this story the leopard, in gratitude, kills game for the hunter; the serpent gives the hunter a snakebite antidote; the rat gives him native cloth, gold dust, and ivory; the man says he's too poor to give a reward. When the man falsely accuses his rescuer of stealing from the king, the hunter saves himself from execution by curing the king's daughter's deadly snakebite, the antidote being mixed, in accordance with the serpent's instructions, with the blood of a traitor—the ungrateful man's. In Tutuola's adaptation the tiger (leopard) promises to provide game; the rat will dig a tunnel to the king's property room and bring Simbi the "properties." The man will watch her farm—and he suggests that Simbi should rescue only him, since the rest of the occupants of the pit are only animals and cannot promise properly. The snake hints that the man is untrustworthy and says that he will help Simbi when she needs help. The leopard and the rat do as they have promised, but the ungrateful man betrays Simbi to the king; she escapes death because the snake, now changed to a gnome, gives her a juju powder (to be mixed with the ungrateful man's blood) which revives the king's dead daughter.

Tutuola's contributions to this story are splendid. The prince warns his father the king about his undignified behavior, climbing up on the partition to look for the missing properties: "But it is very disgraceful for a king like you to climb the partition for yourself in looking for something. If you don't respect yourself, you must respect your office." The terrified royal bell-ringer stays prostrated "with face turned to the floor" while the king smokes and deliberates; the poor bell-ringer is wondering all the while if the king means to "behead him or to send him to somewhere, he never knows which is which." The four obsequious chiefs fall all over themselves for the honor of blowing the first puff of smoke out of the king's pipe, which seems rather sycophantic. The ungrateful man is sought out as if he were a train robber in the American West. The king's "statesmen" print a notice and paste it to every wall and tree: "THE HEAD OF A HUNTER WANTED!" Incidentally, treasure-removing, tunneling friendly creatures are common in African tales. Ogumefu records a tale of ants moving a treasure from the house of a miser who has been hostile to ants to the house of a poor man.[11]

One of the most curious motifs in *Simbi and the Satyr of the Dark Jungle*, Simbi's interrupting herself right in the middle of the word *iromi* (meaning a water insect she has the power to change into), lest she tip off the Satyr to her intentions, has a parallel in a story in the Itayemi-Gurrey collection. In this story a hunter bites off the *tamulibilibi* ("tadpole") to *tamu*, and thereby, like Simbi, saves his life by confusing his enemy. Simbi finally kills the satyr by changing into an *iromi*, flying into the satyr's nostril, and stinging him to death. The fact that she had not "leaked out" all she could do to her enemy had saved her life; the not-so-bright satyr is baffled: "He looked at it for about five minutes. 'This is "iromi" and not "iro . . ." as the lady had mentioned into which she could change." [12]

The rags-to-riches-and-back-again adventures of the Brave African Huntress in the Bachelors' town are rather like the story recorded by the Walkers of the hunter who falls down an alligator hole and is a pampered king in a woman's town until he breaks the taboo by looking into the forbidden room (a Bluebeard motif). The story is rather bare of details in the Walkers' version, whereas Tutuola's is beautifully elaborated. In spite of her being "rough and dirty" and travel-worn, the bachelors, both young and old, are wildly cordial, to say the least: they are "scrambling" her "very greedily" and trying to take her into their houses. When it is arranged among the men that she should choose one of them for a husband, she chooses an old man, "so old and weary that he could not even distinguish man from woman." (She wants to push on to the Jungle of Pigmies and do her duty.) But when the family takes her to the old man's house, a riot breaks out: "a very serious fight started." The marriage project is abandoned; the men take the burrs out of her hair, bathe her, dress her in costly clothes, and crown her queen of their town. Then the "king-makers" tell her that the palace "blongs" to her, but that she must not look into a certain room, whose key they give her. In this room her dirty hair, the burrs, and her rags are wrapped up in a parcel. The new queen's subjects are wonderfully attentive; these cheerful, sociable, wifeless souls visit her all too frequently and must be warned by the palace attendants when they "would open mouth widely and utter—'Ah! this is a lady whom we are longing for to marry!' " Of course she breaks the taboo and enters the forbidden room; a bird throws the parcel on her head, and she comes to in the bush, ragged, dirty, and burr-headed again. Her hesitations before she enters the room are very convincing touches: "When I sat down I continued to think over about the locked room. As I was thinking about it, it was so I was throwing this key up and down and catching it again." [13]

A demon lover story in the Walkers' collection is related to episodes in both *The Brave African Huntress* and *Feather Woman of the Jungle*. In the Walkers' story a hunter wins a beautiful wife by throwing tree seeds into a calabash, but she is a witch, and in the nights she changes into a "mass of teeth" and tries to chew up her husband. Since the hunter's dogs bark loudly each time she tries to eat her husband and so wake him up, the lady persuades him to go hunting with her in the deep forest and leave the dogs chained at home. When they arrive at a suitable spot in the lonely deep forest she changes into the teeth and prepares to eat him. He climbs a tree to escape her (them?). The teeth start chopping the tree down. By magic he makes another tree bend down to pick him up, but the teeth gnaw that tree, and so on. Finally, when he has about run out of trees he begs a passing bird to unchain his dogs at home. The hunter conjures the dogs to the scene of his ordeal, and they eat up the witch wife and lick up the blood.

Tutuola's episode in *Feather Woman of the Jungle* differs from the Walkers' version in significant ways. The demon lover motif is not present at all: there is no trial to win a beautiful witch wife. The chief leaves his dogs home one night when he goes hunting, because he thinks they cannot see in the dark. (His mother insists he should take them, but he "rejects" her advice.) He stops by a rock to rest, falls asleep, and dreams of his previous adventure with the "man who had been transformed into half-snake by his wife." Just then he is knocked on the forehead, slapped, and pushed around by an immortal "night creature," a "tall old woman whose hair is long, dirty, and scattered like that of a mad person and her both breasts were touching the ground." He asks her why she has treated him "so badly like that." After the old hag has "franked both eyes" (squinted at him?) and "murmured with great annoyance" she rants at him for his trespassing in this forest as only Tutuolan ogres and odd creatures can rant. While he is "walking backward with fear," she is pushing him on the nose "with her thick finger"—a comic scene. Not wanting to alert the "savage people" by a gun shot, the chief tries to manage the old hag by poking her on the forehead with the gun butt, but she beats him so "severely" with a stick that he has to climb a tree. But then the hag summons two woodchoppers to cut the tree down (note the more naturalistic treatment here). The chief calls his dogs "with the topmost" of his voice: "My dogs! My dogs! The Cutter, the Sweeper, the Swallower! Let all of you come to this forest now!" (We should note the individualizing touch here.) Back home, the dogs hear their master's voice and they bark and run "to and fro." The mother lets them out, and they run to the tree and drive away the woodcutters and the old woman.

The tree-hopping motif also occurs in an episode of *The Brave African Huntress*. The huntress is under attack from that "super-animal" with the light-producing eyes, none other than the "animal that died but his eyes still alive," whose head the huntress will later use for a sort of searchlight helmet. She is up a tree and the fearful beast is gnawing the tree down. As the tree is about to fall, she jumps to another tree (notice again the naturalistic treatment). After one of Tutuola's lively knock-down-and-drag-out fights, she makes the "super-animal" charge into a tree stump and fasten himself there with his horns, so she can beat him to death with her poisonous cudgel.[14]

Our final parallel shows very clearly Tutuola's great gifts in adapting and elaborating the materials of folk literature. Barker and Sinclair record a rather simple story (from Ghana) illustrating the greediness of the Ashanti trickster hero, Anansi the spider. During a famine Anansi finds a palm tree out on an island. He gets out to the palm tree in a rickety boat, climbs the tree, and tries to drop the palm nuts into the boat below. They all miss the boat and fall into the sea. He dives down for the nuts, and when he reaches the sea bottom, he finds himself before Thunder's pretty cottage. Thunder gives him a magic cooking pot, which is to provide continual food for him and his family. But Anansi, being greedy, keeps the pot in his room for himself. His son finds out about the pot and steals it for the family. Anansi's wife, piqued at her husband's greediness, feeds the whole village with the pot. Unfortunately the pot gets overheated, and melts. To replace the magic pot Anansi goes back to Thunder's cottage on the sea bottom, and Thunder shows the same sympathy as before and gives Anansi a stick. Anxious to try out the magic properties of his new gift he recites the magic formula in his boat. The stick beats him so severely that he has to jump from the boat and swim for shore.

Tutuola's version of this story line is very skillfully elaborated. In a "big and famous town" by a "wide and deep river" the people are suffering terribly from a famine; they are all "as thin as dried stick . . . upper and lower jaws . . . already dried up like a roasted meat." The people are living on cold water, and their "clothes [are] oversized them because they [have] leaned too much." The chief (the narrator) goes out to hunt food for the hungry villagers and for a while he manages to procure a supply of palm nuts, but when the season is over the nuts become very scarce. One day one of the scarce nuts falls out of his canoe and he dives in after it. A kind of scaley, finny, fish-man grabs his legs and takes him down to the bottom of the river in a coffin with a glass lid. The land down there under water is very much like the surface of the earth, except that the sun is dull "like full moon in the dry season" and the air is a little "thicker" than in his home village. On the road to the palace men are lined up "as if they were policemen or soldiers." It's all very convincing; Tutuola uses novelistic techniques to give verisimilitude to a very ancient folk motif. In a beautiful "sitting-room" whose walls are decorated with "stuffed gold fish, polished large sea shells, skulls of the sea animals, etc.," sits the "nymph or the queen of the river." The lady is dressed appropriately in the skins of "beautiful fishes . . . so highly refined that they were as smooth as very costly clothes"; they shine like gold, or twinkle like stars, or sparkle like diamonds. The chief is greatly impressed by the appearance of this nymph: he notices her face "as fresh as that of a fifteen year old," without scars or pimples, her teeth that were "very white and closely to each other," her nose "quite pointed like that of an image," and the "kind and merciful" look to her face. Tutuola, as so often, is entirely successful in making this important folklore character substantial and credible.

While her guardsmen stand by at attention in their shark skull helmets and fish-skin aprons and gloves, carrying four-foot fish tails for weapons, the gracious lady conducts a hearing to investigate the fish-man's charge that the chief has jumped on his head. As the chief answers the lady's questions (asked in her "cool" voice), the guardsmen relax into an "at ease" position, a sign that they are in sympathy with the defendant. After feeding the chief, the nymph gives him a sealed box to provide continual food. He takes the magic box back to the famine town, and feeds the starving population. But soon some "marauders" raid the town and try, unsuccessfully, to get the box, and a second time they succeed by putting honey in the bugles of the king's "bugle-blowers"—making a fine comic scene. Naturally, the chief goes back for another box. The nymph is cross and scolds him, but she gives him a second box. This box produces, not food, but uncountable "bees, wasps, and all kinds of the stinging insects." Many are stung to death, and soon everyone is running "skelter-helter"; even the king makes an undignified exit: while he is "running away for his life," his crown falls off, but he is "unable to wait and take it back." Tutuola always does a fine job of describing such "disordered" scenes, as he calls them. Any reader who wants to be persuaded of Tutuola's literary gifts should compare Tutuola's nicely developed episode with the bare plot as Barker and Sinclair record it.[15]

These are of course only a few of the many, many parallels between tales as recorded in folk tale collections and the developed episodes in Tutuola's novels. The Itayemi-Gurrey volume has other parallels, including some for Drinkard's changing himself into a pebble and throwing himself across a river to escape the "mountain creatures," and the competition in magic between the ghost magician and the wanderer in the Bush of Ghosts. As a matter of fact, virtually any collection of African folk tales—from whatever tribe—is likely to have at least a few parallels to Tutuola episodes. For instance, Drinkard's changing himself into a bird in order to overhear the old man-god tell his wife what the "right thing" was that Drinkard was to bring from the blacksmith, has an analogue in a story told by the Krachi of Togo. Drinkard's pebble transformation also has a parallel in an Ashanti tale from Ghana. Alta Jablow records an Ashanti tale in which a young man has a magic mirror in his hand that allows him to see his home village when he is traveling; this magic mirror is not unlike the extraordinary hand of the Television-handed Ghostess in *My Life in the Bush of Ghosts*. Often the parallels are from very distant peoples. Three Tutuola motifs (Drinkard's rapid-growing baby, his killing a monster from inside his stomach, and his turning himself into a stone) are found in one tale told by the Basuto of South Africa. Another story of a rapid-growing baby comes from the Baronga of Mozambique. These tales have a very wide distribution, and a storyteller in one tribe has access to riches of oral literature far beyond the tribal territory.[16]

Tutuola's novels capture the spirit and manner of the folk tales *as they are actually told*, we might almost say performed. The folk tales as they appear in the collections are usually not much more than bare plot summaries, scenarios for the tales as they are produced before the African audience. They have often been denatured by the moral inhibitions of missionary collectors. The language in them is spoiled: the delightful frolicsome language of the originals has usually been degraded to the tame jargon of educated African narrators. Often they give no idea of the word play or the songs or the rhetorical flourishes of the originals. Probably the collections give an unrepresentative sampling of the types of original stories because certain types do not interest the collectors or violate their sense of propriety.

Of course there is no substitute for the real African storyteller in front of us, miming as well as speaking, changing his voice and his posture to fit the parts, singing the songs that go with the stories, punning and making sly local references.[17] But we do have in Tutuola a storyteller who embellishes the fictional characters and situations as the native storyteller does, who uses a language full of wit and word play and wild humor, not unlike the traditional sort, who freely combines, varies, and rearranges the tales in the manner of the traditional storyteller. And as we have remarked before, Tutuola's language does sound like a speaking voice. In short, Tutuola performs in print something like the function of the native storyteller before his listening audience.

III *Romance versus Realism*

Well, then, Tutuola's ghost novels are indeed folk literature. But does Tutuola's folklore manner constitute a kind of literary betrayal of his country's aspirations for a national literature? Is Tutuola leading the West African novel up a blind alley? Surely he is not; surely it is not wise of educated West Africans to expect their new literature to turn so completely and abruptly from their old literary traditions, whether or not the traditional culture was barbaric and primitive. Mr. E. N. Obiechina argues persuasively that the West African oral tradition will survive for some time: (1) most West Africans are illiterate; (2) "three out of every four West Africans live in traditional village communities or traditional urban settlements"; (3) "even those who are increasingly influenced by the literary culture never lose touch with their oral culture"; and (4) as an embodiment of the "value aspect of a culture" the oral tradition will show "cultural inertia," will be more resistant to change than other areas of the culture.

Why, then, should not the folk tales of the various Nigerian tribes be a good source for one kind of fiction in a new Nigerian literature? This genre would be a poetic romance, perhaps more sophisticated than Tutuola's romances, but, like his, full of "African Gothic" marvels and terrors. The adapting, modifying, sophisticating, expanding, and syncretizing that Tutuola works upon the Yoruba tales suggests that he knows—perhaps in the unconscious way artists often know such things—exactly what he is doing. And what does it matter that the Yoruba folk tales and Tutuola's ghost novels are not realistic? After all, the realistic tradition of the English novel may have been determined by the social conditions of the eighteenth and nineteenth centuries in England; perhaps there is a connection between realism and the commercial standards of the middle class. For all we know, the realistic novel may be something of an exotic in Nigeria. Or perhaps two kinds of long fiction will flourish in Nigeria—the realistic novel and the fantastic romance.

There will be realistic novels, of course; there have been more than a dozen already. By now the realistic novels have had a chance to show their mettle—and, in the opinion of this critic, they have not driven the fantastic romance off the field. Consider the work of Cyprian Ekwensi and Chinua Achebe, the leading Nigerian novelists. Ekwensi's novels (*People of the City, Jagua Nana, Beautiful Feathers* and *Iska*) are lively and graphic evocations of the new Westernized life in Lagos, but they are uncertain in their positive values, as we shall notice when we discuss the attitudes of Nigerian writers toward the old African past. Achebe's novels (*Things Fall Apart, No Longer at Ease, Arrow of Gold* and *A Man of the People*) are so nostalgic about the lost old Ibo culture and so discouraged and fainthearted about the new Nigeria that we may perhaps be forgiven for remembering Tutuola's exuberant good cheer. And at any rate, after we have read Ekwensi, Achebe, Nzekwu and the other Nigerian novelists, Tutuola's strange tales still linger bright and splendid in the memory.[18]

In his classic study *Aspects of the Novel*, E. M. Forster clearly and neatly explains the difficulties many readers have in accepting fantastic characters and incidents. Forster sees that the rejection of fantasy fiction is critically unsound (and this judgment needs to be remembered):

We all know that a work of art is an entity . . . ; it has its own laws which are not those of daily life, anything that suits it is true, so why should questions arise about the angel [typical fantastic character] . . . except whether it is suitable to its book? Why place an angel on a different basis from a stockbroker?

Admitting the validity of this argument Forster confesses that his heart "refuses to assent": he has much sympathy for the rejectors of fantasy. His heart's reason is that our commonest experience with novels has raised expectations that fantasy violates:

The general tone of novels is so literal that when the fantastic is introduced it produces a special effect; some readers are thrilled, others choked off: it demands an additional adjustment because of the oddness of its method or subject matter . . . .[19]

More reading of fantasy fiction, we may suppose, might change such expectations. Is there any reason why our expectations should be rigidly "mimetic" in the novel and not so in the drama? Or perhaps such distinguishing of mimetic and non-mimetic fiction as Frye's, mentioned in Chapter 2, might lead readers to have different kinds of expectations for different kinds of fiction.

One of the paradoxes concerning realism is the fact that a work of fiction that is obviously realistic in the surface details of setting and character may be entirely unrealistic in character motivation or in incidents. On the other hand, fiction which is unrealistic in one or more respects may be in some other respect or respects completely realistic. For instance, the story of Gregor Samsa who wakes up to find himself a gigantic insect with a "hard, as it were, armor-plated, back" and a "dome-like brown belly divided into stiff arched segments on top of which the bed quilt could hardly keep in position," certainly violates the canons of factual truth, but it is entirely realistic about the conditions of work of small bureaucrats in our highly organized modern way of life and about their oppressed, alienated souls.[20]

Likewise, as we have already observed, Tutuola's heroes and heroines display realistically a certain rather narrow range of human motivations. Besides this realism of character motivation, all the romances have realistic touches here and there. A reader who finds it hard to believe that Tutuola is ever realistic might examine these episodes—and this rather extensive list could be made even longer: the fading away and estrangement of Drinkard's friends when the palm-wine is no longer forthcoming, the skull's harsh words to his foolish lover (Drinkard's wife-to-be), the irresponsible and disorderly conduct of the hungry crowd fed by Drinkard's magic egg, the wanderer in the Bush of Ghosts getting drunk at his wedding and treading on a small ghost, the flies gathering on the wanderer when he is a god in a pitcher, his quarrel with his wife Super Lady about bringing up their son, the buyers' bribing of the auctioneer at the sale of Simbi, Simbi's friends' acidulous comments on her wish to know the "punishments" of life, the African Huntress leaning bewildered against a tree after she has lost the paradise of Bachelors' town, the grumbling of the unfaithful wife's lover when she keeps him waiting at a tryst, and the mad clamor of the people of the famine town when the narrator of *Feather Woman of the Jungle* hesitates to go back for a second magic food-producing box. Actually, Tutuola has considerable powers in realism.[21] And some of Tutuola's readers might insist that his works treat realistically the terrors of the subconscious, or even that they present, in their malice-and-hostility-filled visions, a realistic picture of man's essentially fearful and absurdly hopeless position in the universe. It is probably safer and less confusing, however, to think of Tutuola as a non-realistic writer, telling what he has to tell about human life in ways other than the ways of the realists.

IV *Tutuola and Fagunwa*

If educated West Africans admit that folk tales are proper sources for modern African literature, they usually say that Fagunwa has used the sources more artistically. It must be admitted that Tutuola was not the first to write extended romances based on Yoruba folk tales. Since 1949 the Yoruba writer D. O. Fagunwa has written a number of romances in classical Yoruba based on folk materials. These romances are much admired by educated Yoruba-speakers; indeed, among these Yoruba it is a sort of critical commonplace that Tutuola is merely doing in English, which he cannot write properly, what Fagunwa did much better in a beautiful, correct Yoruba, and that Tutuola is writing to Europeans and so lays on the exoticism thick to confirm the European image of Africa, whereas Fagunwa is addressing African readers much as a traditional African storyteller would.

Without knowing Yoruba we cannot tell whether Fagunwa was more successful than Tutuola in adapting folk tales for extended romances, though we may distrust the educated Yoruba critics' judgment somewhat because of their blindness to Tutuola's merits. We may take on faith the beauty of Fagunwa's classical Yoruba language, and still admire Tutuola's admittedly very unclassical English. We might admit that Tutuola was not addressing Africans exclusively, but we would deny that he was writing for Europeans exclusively or that he was catering to European prejudice about Africa. If relatively few Africans read Tutuola's works, the reasons would be the high cost of his books, as compared with the Onitsha pamphlets, for instance, and the bad press they got from educated African readers. We might add that it is not necessarily disloyal, in an ecumenical age, to address oneself to the English-speaking world.

Perhaps Tutuola got the "general idea" from Fagunwa—the creation of folk romances out of the traditional Yoruba story materials. Perhaps some of Tutuola's vivid descriptions—of *outré* monsters, for instance—owe something to Fagunwa's work. We might suppose, further, that Tutuola was encouraged in his bent for multiple-magic-wielding heroes, stupendous battles with monsters, wildly imaginative creatures and events, and the inventive use of language (with exuberant similes) by the example of a literary artist who has been immensely popular in Yorubaland.

But would it not be reasonable to admire *both* writers rather than one at the expense of the reputation of the other? We might admire Fagunwa, as Ulli Beier suggests, for his humor, his effective rhetoric (like the rhythmical, climactic repetitions), his word play, his "bizarre" imagery, his "shrewd and detailed observations of real life" —qualities which have endeared Fagunwa to his compatriots but which Westerners also might appreciate. Then we might make distinctions. We might prefer Tutuola's cool matter-of-factness to Fagunwa's occasional sentimentality and frequent moralizing. On the other hand, we might agree with Beier's judgment that Fagunwa surpasses Tutuola "as an observer of the Yoruba mind at work." We might prefer Tutuola's more authentic Yoruba materials or Fagunwa's mixture of inventions and traditional materials.[22] When Soyinka's translation of a Fagunwa novel is available we will be better able to assess the relationship between Tutuola and Fagunwa, but admiring them both seems a good solution now.

CHAPTER 4

Mythological Thinking

E VEN if educated West Africans were persuaded of the originality
of Tutuola's work, they would, we may presume, still object
strenuously to his "immersion in the mythical past with its gods,
ghosts, wars, sacrifices, and submerged terrors"; they feel that such
a preoccupation "delays progress." [1] We might admit the truth of
this charge and then say that the extenuating circumstances are more
important than the charge itself. In this chapter, we will notice the
kind and degree of Tutuola's "immersion in the mythical past." Then
in the next chapter we will assess the social danger of such mythologizing and try to find reasons for the educated West Africans' excessive worrying on the subject.

I The "Old" Africa

It is true that one of the most conspicuous qualities of Tutuola's
ghost novels is the pristine, pre-contact, old African atmosphere of
them. None of the five novels has a white character or explicitly
mentions a white person. *Simbi and the Satyr of the Dark Jungle*
and *The Brave African Huntress* make no mention of Western institutions, unless an auction with a "touting man" in *Simbi* would
qualify, or the "custody" and the "pesters" in *The Brave African
Huntress*, which do vaguely suggest Nazi concentration camps and
cruel Nazi guards. [2] The Africa of all five novels is substantially the
old-time Africa of communal working in the king's fields, cowrie
shell money, interminable lawsuits, powerful priest-kings and their
councils, polygamy, slavery, tribal wars, and frequent human sacrifice. That is to say, these conditions characterize the human events
of the novels. The ghostly events of the novels are not so easily placed
in time. Ogres and ogresses, fantastic transformations and incredibly
powerful juju belong to the age of the persons that believe in such
things, and although that would generally be old-time Africa before

the arrival of the whites, it could also be some time in our century. In Joyce Cary's novel *Aissa Saved* (1932) based on his experience as a political officer in Nigeria, the villagers of Kolu are persuaded that Aissa has turned into a yellow she-dog; an old woman "swore that Aissa had changed before her eyes and caught up Abba [her baby] in her teeth to gallop away with her." [3] Cary's African novels contain dozens of such incidents.

The time setting of Tutuola's novels can be determined with some precision: it is pretty certainly the nineteenth century. That century did indeed bring to Yorubaland "many kinds of African wars . . . general wars, tribal wars, burglary wars and the slave wars." [4] Around 1810 the great Yoruba state of Oyo, once dominant over a wide area in western Nigeria and Dahomey, began to disintegrate. Provincial chiefs defied the authority of the alafin of Oyo, and tributary states refused any longer to acknowledge Oyo suzerainty. The Moslem Fulani of the north intervened in this disintegration and overran the country as far south as Abeokuta. The result of this time of troubles was that the northern parts of the state became subject to Fulani emirs, and the southern chiefs became entangled in a devastating series of civil wars lasting for nearly a century.

This social disorder encouraged slave-raiding, as did the presence of Europeans in the nearby ports of Badagri and Lagos, eager to sell guns and buy slaves. Amos Tutuola's own town of Abeokuta was a gathering place for refugees who sought safety in the general anarchy and lust for slaving of southern Yorubaland. Educated West Africans should see in Tutuola's novels a certain kind of grim political realism. It must be admitted that Tutuola's fictional nineteenth century Yorubaland ought to have a few whites in it, for the Church Missionary Society (Church of England) established a mission in Abeokuta in 1844, and the Methodists followed soon afterwards. (The gun-running and slaving were probably done through native middlemen.) [5]

Perhaps there is *one* white person in the ghost novels, though she is not explicitly recognized as such—Faithful-Mother in the White Tree. Faithful-Mother is simply described as an "old woman," but her establishment, which is a kind of combination missionary compound and hotel or night club, looks like a white person's establishment of the twentieth century. [6] In *Feather Woman* a curious reference to white men—a sort of mythological reference—mentions the "two foot marks" which belonged to "the first white men who had traveled from heaven through that rock to the earth." These footprints, or shoe prints, are one of the sights to be seen in Ife, the sacred city of Yorubaland.[7]

II *Magic*

But to be really impressed with the pristine Africanness of Tutuola's novels one must hear something of his folklore marvels: the magical juju powers, especially the transformations. No more than the traditional Yoruba tale teller is Tutuola cribbed and confined in his literary imagination by such considerations as the dicta of logic, the literary canons of plausibility, or the scientific truths of vertebrate anatomy and physics. We can readily imagine that Tutuola's magical marvels are so many affronts to the positivistic and progressive creed of educated West Africans.

Besides transformations mentioned elsewhere, Drinkard twice changes himself into a lizard, he dissolves into air, twice changes into a very big bird and once into a very small bird like a sparrow, and also changes into a great fire. He changes his wife into a kitten and a wooden doll. Among the almost "uncountable" marvels so flagrantly unscientific are the cowrie shell that makes the future Mrs. Drinkard dumb (a real miracle!), "crops that grow in five minutes and ripen in ten," the bush that smells like baking pastry and roasting meats, the road that will not let Drinkard and his wife stop or "branch" or turn back, and the drum that "beats himself up into heaven." [8]

Some other marvels in this romance are Skull, with his rented body parts, a "half-bodied baby" born from his mother's left thumb, the headless, limbless living white pillar, the "tiny creature" who makes weeds grow up instantly, the ground too hot to stand on, the Red-people in Red-town, the belligerent dead babies marching to Deads' Town, the juice with which the "huge creature" revived his dead followers, and the magic egg that feeds a multitude.[9]

Of the old-time African marvels of *My Life in the Bush of Ghosts* many are practiced by Smelling-Ghost, the chief transformation artist in the romance: he changes the hero into a monkey, a lion, a horse, and a cow. Super Lady, also adept in this technique, changes herself into an antelope, a lioness, a boa constrictor, a tigress, and a goat. To mention only a few of the hero's feats of magical derring-do, he can smoke a six-foot pipe burning half a ton of tobacco at a time, can fly (on top of a coconut tree), and can fashion from mud a new arm for the one-armed wife of a king. The silverish ghost can, with his silver light, "transparent" a person, presumably like a fluoroscope.

Invisible Pawn is able to revive dead warriors, even when he has to replace cut-off heads. A certain small ghost can raise "the cover of his eye" and light up the bush like daylight.[10] Some lesser marvels in this romance are the judicious, arbitrating ghosts' ability to listen to what the narrator's "heart is saying," as if a telegraphist were sending a message; newly born babies smelling like dead animals; a talking land that complains of being trod on; an ugly ghostess whose ugliness irresistibly attracts the narrators; the "fire creatures" who "barb" their clients with "scissors of fire"; women with long brown moustaches; the inhabitants of Hopeless-town, who talk with a "shrug language"; a "jocose-ghostess," whose jokes would cure the sick; a bridge so slight it must be crossed naked; the Invisible Missive Magnetic Juju to bring a lost person home; and a magic contest in which the narrator transforms himself into a stick, rain, a big fish, a bird, and air.[11]

Although *Simbi and the Satyr of the Dark Jungle* is comparatively sparing in magic, the redoubtable Simbi overcomes her antagonist the Satyr by changing herself into an iromi insect, flying into his nostril and there stinging him to death. She is able to blind her husband with a curse and the Satyr with a slap. And she has considerable magical aid from well-wishers: a grateful snake, who later becomes a gnome and saves her life by giving her a powder to revive a dead princess, and three "gods" in her satchel, who provide rain, lightning, a flood, and a locust plague to help her when she is surrounded by the Satyr and his followers.[12]

The Brave African Huntress is moderate in magic. Aside from a magical snakebite antidote which the Huntress has taken before she left home, and a juju compass (a cow's tail that points in the "right direction"), Adebesi pretty much relies on her superlative natural powers. Most of the magic is accomplished by the several monsters in the novel, which (or whom) we will consider later. In the one metamorphosis of the novel, Adebesi becomes the pampered queen of Bachelors' town and is later transformed back into her previous dirty, ragged, travel-worn self, after she, like Bluebeard's wife, wishes to look into a forbidden place. The very entertaining incident of the Ibembe king's horns, the buried secret, and the talkative bugle is perhaps the most extravagant magic in the novel. Incidentally, Tutuola has assured the writer that this story, so reminiscent of Ovid's Midas story (in "Wife of Bath's Tale," III, 591 ff.) is in fact based on Yoruba sources.[13]

Though *The Feather Woman of the Jungle* is not as crowded with marvels as the first two romances, the book is scarcely in the realistic mode. Besides the considerable magical capacities of the Feather Woman, the unfaithful queen, the warriors of the Diamond Goddess, and the Hairy Giantess of the underworld, to be detailed under the heading of Tutuolan monstrosity, there are a number of fairly impressive violations of the natural order. The narrator's dogs "Sweeper, Cutter, and Swallower" seem to have preternatural hearing: locked in a room, they hear their master calling from a treetop deep in the bush. The king of the "savage men" has a voice that shakes the "hills, rocks, and trees," and terrifies the jungle animals into silence. When the narrator dives into the river for a lost palm fruit, a fish-man drags him down through the water in a glass coffin and takes him to an underwater land, whose queen gives the narrator a magic food-producing box to relieve a famine-stricken village and later, a replacement for that box, which produces "bees, wasps and other stinging insects." In their sight-seeing in the Yoruba sacred city of Ife, the narrator and his men see "the footmarks of the first white men who had traveled from heaven to the world," the lane (magically weedless and swept) by which the founder of the Yoruba tribe went back to heaven, and "the wells from which the sun and the moon are rising into the sky." In Ede the narrator and his men meet and shake hands with Sango the thunder god and his wife; the thunder god obligingly makes a thunderstorm for them by shaking pebbles in a gourd; Sango gives the party transformation pills and his wife gives them pills to change themselves back again. Later, the narrator and his party descend into the underworld through a house "narrow and as long as a chimney," apparently rather like a pit head above a mine.[14]

III   *Tutuolan Monstrosity*

Experienced readers know that it is possible for a realistic literary character to bore one by a kind of drabness and humdrum mediocrity. Tutuola's ogres, or monsters, though they violate natural laws outrageously in their appearances, their constitutions, and their actions, have human interest, and they are "living" in a sense meaningful to literary criticism, just as Dickens' so-called caricatures have a literary vitality that has delighted millions for two centuries. And Tutuola's monsters are delightful creations of humor, wit, and fancy; indeed they are one of his fortes.

The monsters that Drinkard meets are pretty *outré*, even more so than those in the traditional Yoruba tales. Out of a very full collection of monsters in this novel, these specimens have especially entertained one connoisseur of monstrosity: the lion-headed Spirit of Prey, as big as a hippopotamus and covered with scales as big as a shovel, able to "focus" his prey so that it drops dead and then drags itself to him; Faithful-Mother's huge white tree with a pair of clutching hands and a voice that sounds as if "many persons talked into a tank"; and the red fish that (minotaur-like) exacts a tribute of human sacrifices from the Red-people, that has a head like a tortoise's but as large as an elephant's, and has thirty horns spread out like an umbrella over his long stringy red hair.[15]

The old-time African-style monsters in *My Life in the Bush of Ghosts* are possibly more numerous, extravagant, and flamboyant than those of the first novel. Perhaps the most repulsive monster is Smelling-Ghost (that is, Stinking Ghost): "All kinds of snakes, centipedes, and flies were living on every part of his body," and his body was befouled with excreta, urine, and the "rotten blood of all the animals that he was killing for his food." But for all the gruesome charms of Smelling-Ghost and other monsters in the romance (like the Rev. Devil who baptizes with fire and hot water, the ghost with the watery eyes, the snake that vomits colored lights, the cannibalistic grave robber, the Television-handed Ghostess covered with maggoty sores, and the hero himself as a long-necked god in a jug), the most spectacular monster is the flash-eyed mother.

This hydra-headed female is immense and immobile, "fill[s] the town as a vast round hill," and "does not move to anywhere at all." Besides her own huge head, visible four miles from town, covered with a great mop of dirty hair full of birds' nests (the influence of Joyce Kilmer's "Trees"?), she has millions of small heads all over her body, making a mighty racket, "arguing, flogging, and reporting themselves to their mother." The flash-eyed mother executes those who displease her by flashing fire out of "two fearful large eyes" in her principal head.[16]

Simbi and the Satyr of the Dark Jungle is sparing—but only relatively sparing—in monsters. The second title character is a rather unpleasant-looking fellow, a ten-foot giant who lights up the area when he "goggles both eyes." Dressed only in a bloody apron covered with dead birds' heads, unkempt with "dirty long hair" and floor-sweeping beard, he is "a pessimist," and an "impatient and ill-tempered, impenitent and noxious creature." The Satyr is moderately competent in juju; besides less impressive feats like "vomiting" a bottle and putting Simbi inside it "by force," he fashions by magic an "illusive" concert hall, its walls, windows, and roof made of living birds whose plumage is of pure gold, a concert hall with an orchestra eager to play what Simbi wants to sing and a *corps de ballet* eager to dance with her, but, also ominously, a guard squad of white-shoed, white-masked ostriches to prevent her escape. The second most important monster is Bako, whose strange seizures of hostility are caused by her identical twin's behavior at home, and whose transformation into a "cockish lady" (that is, rooster) constitutes one of the most striking of Tutuola's African metamorphoses.[17]

The Brave African Huntress is rather more generous in monsters than the previous novel. The jungle giant Odara, a long-haired, pimply-faced worthy with "knots" and scars all over his body, catches bullets fired at him and *eats them*. The bald, bearded pigmy "gatekeeper" with thick arms, thick legs, and thick veins (varicose?) is also proof against gun-shot. The "bad semi-bird," who tears open roofs and snatches the terrified victims, can talk like a human. One of the pigmy outpost guards, a "huge and short" chap with big banana-shaped fingers, a big belly "sounding heavily," and a big goitre, cuts off the huntress' left foot "unexpectedly" and then later puts it back on again, as good as new. "Super-animal," an elephant-sized, horned, long-haired fright that *scares* his prey to death, has eyes that emit a "powerful light"—even after death.[18]

The chief monsters of *The Feather Woman of the Jungle,* which is rather economical of monsters, are the Feather Woman herself, the Treacherous Queen, the formidable troopers of the Goddess of Diamonds, and Hairy Giant and Giantess. The Feather Woman, the most interesting of these scary creatures, goes about surrounded by a crowd of "more than two hundred small and big birds," including a huge ostrich which stays very close to her (all the birds are enchanted persons). She is covered with feathers which "were really grown out from her body," her eyes are "red and hollow with age," and she is toothless, "so that made her mouth be moving up and down as if she was eating something in the mouth." Hapless wanderers who accidentally "trespass" her jungle and offend her she transforms into "images" (who still have feeling) and whips them mercilessly and regularly, "snorting . . . repeatedly and with her snappishness . . . scorning and abusing them." [19]

The two stout warriors that the Goddess of Diamonds sends to abduct her daughter Sela, who has eloped with the narrator, are passing strange personages. One is an archer dressed in silver armor ornamented with diamonds. He rides a camel; a tall hat grotesquely decorated with sea animals and fish skulls masks his face. The other one is armed with a diamond cudgel, dressed in leather armor ornamented with fish and reptile bodies. His hat is decorated with four animal heads facing in four directions; all the heads seem alive. Besides their human prowess with the bow and arrow and the diamond cudgel, and their apparent power to cause an earthquake and a big fog, one of them (which one is unspecified) shouts "greatly with a kind of a voice," bringing a thunderstorm whose lightning breaks the window of the narrator's house, enters the house, and sets fire to it, thus driving Sela and her husband out into the open, where Sela is eventually caught and carried off.[20]

The Hairy Giant and his wife the Hairy Giantess are splendid Tutuolan monsters, top-drawer specimens in a Tutuolan specialty. This precious oversized pair (twelve feet tall) are naked, and their bodies are covered with hair "fluffy as that of a cat." The hair on their heads is so bushy that their heads look immense, and the long hair on their feet makes their feet look as though they had shoes on them. Their mouths are "hardly to see" for the hair which almost hides them. Their eyes are more prominent, the eyeballs being "swelled out like a big knob of a tree." Their noses are "very big" and their nostrils are full of hair.

The Giant carries a cudgel so big that he must rest it on his shoulder. His wife carries a dead antelope in one hand and a dead hawk in the other. When the narrator and his party approach this grisly underworld couple, the Giant bellows out a Tutuola-style monster's battle boast:

Who are you? Who are you eating my mangoes? Stop in one place and let your death meets [sic] you there or be running away and let your death chase you! Please, choose neither [either] of the two! Because I am the death who is coming to kill you all now! Willing or not all of you will go in my soup pot tonight!

When the monstrous pair capture the narrator and his men, the giantess paralyzes them all by looking "sternly" at them, and the Giant and his wife torture the narrator and his party by putting them, tied up, close to a fire burning pepper. Finally the monsters prepare to roast the victims for supper. Naturally the narrator escapes from his bonds and, after a terrific conflict, manages to disable the monsters by pushing them into a river.[21]

Incidentally, these flamboyant monsters, together with the wild transformations, have suggested to some readers, including this writer, that Tutuola's romances would make effective Disney fantasies. As a matter of fact, Walt Disney Productions has considered making a movie of Tutuola's works and perhaps has not yet entirely given up the idea. And in July of 1964 a representative of Tutuola's publisher reported that an American film company had bought the film rights to *The Palm-Wine Drinkard*.[22]

Monsters are more prominent in Tutuola's work than they are in his Yoruba sources. It is tempting to speculate on the reason for this "monstrosity" in his vision. Northrop Frye has suggested the relevance of such speculation for the romance:

> Translated into dream terms, the quest-romance is the search of the libido or desiring self for a fulfillment that will deliver it from the anxieties of reality but still contain that reality. The antagonists of the quest are often sinister figures, giants, ogres, witches, and magicians, that clearly have a parental origin; and yet redeemed and emancipated parental figures are involved too, as they are in the psychological quests of Freud and Jung.[23]

Do they represent Jung's mother figures, father figures, the shadow, the animal, the Wise Old Man, the childish figures of innocence? [24] Are Tutuola's ogres and witches Jungian archetypes? Perhaps the flash-eyed mother, Feather Woman, the Goddess of Diamonds, and the Hairy Giantess are ogreish mother figures, and Faithful-Mother a benign mother figure.[25] Perhaps Smelling-Ghost and the Satyr of the Dark Jungle are malignant father figures.[26] Going beyond Frye's concerns, we might suppose that such minor ogres as the "hungry-creature," "Odara," the "giant-like or cyclops-like creature," "obstacle" (with the "half fall goitre"), and the "huge stern pigmy" (with the outsized navel) are Shadow figures, representing Tutuola's unconscious notion of his worst side.[27] Perhaps also Super Lady, the Television-handed Ghostess, Bako the "Siamese" twin, the Treacherous Queen, and the Queen of the River are *anima* figures, or images of the eternal feminine. It may be that the archetype that Jung calls the Wise Old Man, a helper in the quest, is exemplified in the snake-and-gnome that saves Simbi from death and by the dried "slender stick" of an old man who "interviews" and blesses travelers at the gatehouse for the underworld; significantly, this type of character is rare in Tutuola's romances.[28]

Although Jung suggests that children may be images of innocence, in Tutuola's romances even the children are sometimes malevolent. The monstrous child born out of Drinkard's wife's left thumb is a monumental pest; he is such a voracious eater, furious smasher of things, and brawler that when the villagers see "his havocs and bad character" they insist that he be exiled. The fierce dead babies marching on the road to Deads' Town at "two o'clock in the midnight" drive Drinkard and his wife off the road.[29]

Ulli Beier has offered a simple explanation of Tutuola's "monstrosity": "To a Christian and half-educated man, Yoruba tradition would obviously look more frightening, monstrous, and grotesque than to somebody in that culture." [30] That is, Tutuola's monstrous vision reflects the missionary horror of the indigenous religious cultures. Beier's explanation is plausible, but does it really explain enough? Does it explain why most of Tutuola's supernatural figures are malevolent? Although amateur psychologists ought to be very, very tentative about such recondite matters as Jungian archetypes, the archetypes do seem suggestive as explanations of Tutuola's monsters.

IV *Western Elements*

But in spite of this old-time pre-contact African setting of the folk novels, white man's customs, institutions, techniques, and instruments make their appearance in the most interesting way. In *The Palm-Wine Drinkard,* for instance, guns and bottles are mentioned (such trade goods were brought up from the European coastal "factories" in the nineteenth century). Faithful-Mother in the white tree looks rather like a strangely indulgent missionary and her establishment like a combination mission compound and luxury hotel or night club. When Drinkard and his wife meet her she is sitting "on a chair in a big parlour which was decorated with costly things." Faithful-Mother's establishment has a dance hall with "twenty stages," "uncountable orchestras," and some sort of display of "images," apparently photographs of the guests, including Drinkard and his wife, lights "in technicolour" "changing colour at five minutes interval." In Faithful-Mother's dining hall free food and drinks are available to the guests day and night, provided by three hundred and forty cooks; the dining hall seems to be managed by a "chief waiter." There is a hospital, where Drinkard and his wife have their injured heads "tended to" and a room "to be play gamble," where Drinkard loses the money he gained by selling his and his wife's death. When Drinkard and his wife leave, Faithful-Mother gives

Drinkard a gun and ammunition and a cutlass, and provides the couple with roasted meats, drinks, and *cigarettes*.[31]

Soon after they have left Faithful-Mother, Drinkard and his wife meet the ten-foot-high "Red-lady," who is dressed in Western-style high fashion, "in a long fancy gown, and there were many gold beads around her neck and she wore high-heel shoes which resembled aluminum in colour." In one of the two judicial dilemmas Drinkard is asked to render a judgment on, the quarreling wives of the revived husband are arrested in the Western style: "unluckily a police-man was passing by that time and he arrested them and charged them to the court." Drinkard, describing the increase in the crowd of persons expecting to be fed by his magic food-producing egg brought from the Deads' Town, observes that they had "increased by 60 per-cent." [32]

My Life in the Bush of Ghosts reflects most this syncretism of the old Africa and the new Westernization. The wanderer in the Bush of Ghosts marries his first wife in a church wedding with a best man (who's been punished in the fire of hell more than fifty years) and a reception afterwards. The pastor of the sort of anti-church in which the marriage takes place is Rev. Devil; "Traitor" reads the lesson, and "Judas" closes the service. When the wanderer gives his "earthly name," the evil congregation insist that he be baptized; their baptism is done with "fire and hot water." But this Westernized episode has an African finale. At the reception "Spirit of Prey" and "Skull" get into a fight much enjoyed by hand-clapping wedding guests, and when "an old ape who was a slave" beats on a hollow tree as if on a drum, the whole wedding party—"ghosts, evils, terrible creatures," and himself—can't bear to "wait or stand still," but start dancing; the wanderer is rather drunk and stamps on a small ghost, which offense could have cost him fifty years of imprisonment.

The wanderer's second wife, Super Lady, lives in a very elegant European-style house complete with bathroom (no running water apparently, but "as clean as a food plate"), dressing room, bedroom, parlor with an "easy chair with cushions, and full length mirror," and kitchen and dining room. As though she were the wife of a senior service official, she has two maids; and she and her husband enjoy such Western amenities as soap with a "lofty" smell, sponges, tea, bread, and iced drinks. She dresses her husband in "costly clothes as trousers, shirt, tie, socks, hat, golden ring with . . . costly wrist-watch," to match her own Western get-up, "underwear, gown, golden beads, rings, hat, shoes, wrist-watch" and hand-bag. However, Super Lady is not *quite* the typical fashionable lady of the West: she is not a human, of course, but a "ghostess"; she is capable of changing herself into animals (an antelope, a lioness, a boa constrictor, and a bird), and she is the daughter of the leading witch and wizard of all the earthly and ghostly towns, a precious couple who had meant to sacrifice their own daughter. (Super Lady's grandmother is presently in the "everlasting fire.")[33]

The wanderer's dead cousin, in the tenth town, has brought the "Christianity works" to this town of ghosts: he has founded the Methodist Church of the Bush of Ghosts, a school where ghost children learn "to read and write and also scripture which is the main subject," a one-man extension school to teach "sanitary work, surveying, building, and first aid nursery work." Having trained "many bright scholars as teachers and headmasters," he has founded "over a thousand churches with schools in provinces which are under this tenth town," and has persuaded the ghostly town fathers to introduce "new plans of houses." With the help of the Synod and his corps of supervisors, directors of education, and education officers, he is supervising this vast ecclesiastical-educational establishment as the bishop of the diocese (in a dream a voice from heaven has ordained him bishop). The dead cousin's wife, a Zulu lady doctor, is director of medical services, treats patients in the town's hospitals, trains nurses and medical officers. Medicines and medical equipment, books and stationery, and building materials are furnished by dead "medicine-makers" and "hospital apparatus-makers," dead publishers, and dead building supply merchants.

After learning how to read and write and being tutored by his dead cousin in "how to be acting as a dead man," the wanderer goes off to the "Deads' Town" to learn "how to judge cases" and "also all the branches of the court works." When he finishes this training he puts his learning to use: builds police stations, courts, and prison yards, trains young people in police and court work, and finally becomes judge of the highest court. At this time the new judge gives his cousin some advice on how to marry off his four daughters to "earthly" men; he suggests that the cousin advertise in the earthly newspapers!

This whole episode is a revealing little capsule history of missionary activities in a Nigerian town. But the episode is not completely Westernizing in its approach: the hospitality and the recreation at his cousin's look very African—the prominent ghosts sending food and drinks to his cousin's compound, the "dancing, drumming, and singing the song of ghosts until daybreak." There is one note of the African-mythological, for some of the ghost guests danced in such a way until they "cut into halves and both these halves were also dancing." [34]

Some other Western institutions, jobs, and objects mentioned in this romance, besides the many Westernized figures of speech, are an exhibition (of smells!), a conference (of ghosts; they "like to be in conference at all times"), functions (a "birthday function" and a "bad-bye" function, parties), an "incognito lawyer," a carpenter and the "solid coffin" he makes, a "resurrectionist" (grave-robber, but this one is a cannibal too), an alarm whistle, guns, a strike, clippers, scissors, and knives (for "barbing"), a guard of honor, a "notice-board" (sign), and television (the TV screen in the hand of the Television-handed Ghostess). The "invisible magnetic missile" is Western only in name; it refers to the hometown fortune-teller's power of remote control over the dreams of the wanderer, to make him want to come home again from the tenth town. [35]

In *Simbi and the Satyr of the Dark Jungle* and *The Brave African Huntress* Western elements are—unaccountably—much rarer. *Simbi* has only a "weighing scale," an auctioneer and his "touting man," a shotgun, a makeshift stretcher, "necroses," a big bottle ("vomited" by the satyr), an "illusive" concert hall and white shoes (on the "hoofs" of ostrich guards!). If the gnome, the satyr, the phoenix are Western in origin, they are Africanized almost out of recognition: the satyr, for instance, is rather more like Al Capp's Hairless Joe than the shaggy-haired nymph-chasers of classical mythology, and the gnome, though he lives underground in the approved European manner, performs the tricks of a traditional Yoruba animal hero like Tortoise. The phoenix seems to have no powers of rebirth; she *dies* in a fire rather than being reborn in one. She reminds us of a German Stuka divebomber rather than the classical bird. Imps, gnomes, and goblins are noted in passing, without comment or description, as part of the Satyr's hellish crew. However, a pitiless slave overseer is fittingly called a "myrmidon," that is, a loyal and ruthless subordinate. When Simbi calls out from inside the hollow tree, the woodchopper's son appropriately wonders if she is "a human or a nymph." [36]

The Brave African Huntress mentions a "shaka-bullah gun" (named for its noise "shaka—bul—laha"), which may be the rather primitive dane gun imported from Europe in the nineteenth century, a "juju compass" which is a cow's tail, gunpowder, "special concerts" (provided for the Queen of Bachelors' town), and chocolates and ice cream, mentioned in the boatmen's improvised song. Mentioned in passing as "curious creatures" which the Huntress' father has "fought and conquered" are these classical Western importations: elves, genii, goblins, demons, imps, and gnomes. These creatures are not described, and they play no part in the story. Perhaps the big "half fall goitre" of the pigmy called "obstacle" owes something to Western medical science, and the "reflecting eyes" of the "super animal" which produce "the clear and broad light" are a fantasy version of floodlights. The "custody" and its "pesters" remind us of Nazi concentration camps and Nazi guards. But most of the limited number of Western elements are found in similes. This romance and *Simbi and the Satyr of the Dark Jungle,* as we indicated above, has the most thoroughly old-African atmosphere.[37]

It is hard to say why it should be so, but Western objects and customs are much more evident in *Feather Woman of the Jungle* than in the two previous romances. The following Western items are mentioned: "farm" jumpers, expensive dresses, a gun, "some shots of drink," snow, a steeple (on top of a tower!), a "beautiful storey [apartment house?] that had many flats," living quarters with an "ornamented arm chair," a bathroom (running water not mentioned), a sitting room, and "house cleaners." The Queen of the River, who is very much Westernized, has guardsmen who seem to stand at attention and at ease, slippers, and as decorations on her walls, stuffed fish—gold fish! The narrator approaches her underwater realm in what might be considered a Western object: a coffin with a glass lid. Another potentate visited by the narrator has a number of appurtenances that may owe something to Western jewelry: "diamond seats and decorations," "diamond statues," "diamond uniforms," and the lady's own diamond dress. This lady's "rest room" is not as Western as it seems; it is probably a private room to rest in. The expressions "trespassed my jungle," and "monopolized people of their property" are interesting African reflections on Western private property and finance capitalism. As in *Drinkard,* the curious use of percentiles occurs; the crowd gathering to listen to the narrator increases "by seventy-five per cent" and later "by more than ninety per cent." [38]

But one of the most interesting aspects of Tutuola's syncretism is his use of Western technology and Western customs to make figures of speech, usually similes. This practice is most common in the first two romances. When the lady who will later be Drinkard's wife tries to escape from her husband, the skull, and his relatives chase her, they are "rolling on the ground as if a thousand petrol drums were pushing along a hard road." Drinkard's "half-bodied baby" talks "with a lower voice like a telephone." To escape from some highwaymen and boa constrictors he employs one of his jujus and becomes "a big bird like an airplane." The beams of light coming out of the eyes of "Spirit of Prey" produce a "floodlight like mercury in color." Faithful-Mother gives Drinkard and her other guests a magical self-refilling wine bottle "exactly the size of injection bottle." The horrible red fish's multiple eyes open and close "as if a man was pressing a switch off and on." The "nine terrible creatures" with voices like a church bell and bodies "cold as ice" have "skin as sharp as sandpaper." [39]

The wanderer in the Bush of Ghosts finds a sunken doorway in a hillside, and its portico shines "as if it was polished with Brasso at all moments." Beyond the Brasso-polished portico, the underground home of the golden ghost, the "copperish" ghost, and the "silverish" ghost, the wanderer is so wrought up over a ghostly quarrel over him that his heart is "throbbing repeatedly as if a telegraphist is sending messages by telegraph." When the wanderer is "corked tightly" in a hollow log his muffled outcries sound like "lofty music" to the "homeless ghosts" who are listening to the noise-making log "as a radio." Evil-of-Evils' handshake shocks like a "live electric wire." When he is a long-necked "god" with his body jammed into a pitcher, his pipe puffs out smoke "as if smoke is rushing from a big boiler." He observes that the flash-eyed mother's eyes can ignite firewood "like petrol or other inflammable spirit or gunpowder," and that they light up her town "like electricity." When the wanderer screams with pain from having been burnt by the flash-eyed mother's flame-throwing, the short ghosts, her cohorts, laugh "as if uncountable cannons fired together" and the flash-eyed mother's own laughter sounds "as if a bomb explodes." When the flash-eyed mother and the million hydra-like baby heads are eating all at once, their mouths make "noises as if one hundred winches were going at the same time." [40]

These Westernizing similes, especially the technological ones, have considerable graphic vigor. They give a rather curious effect, as though Tutuola were leading his compatriots out of their acculterating, Westernizing world, with its ready acceptance of Western technology, back into the old mythical world of heart's desire and heart's terror, or as though Tutuola were making the reader dream an old African nightmare and the technical figures were merely remnants of the mechanical paraphernalia of waking life. Of course, like the other Western items we have observed, they are anachronistic, but somehow the reader never notices, or if he does, he doesn't care; Tutuola's romances are not realistic literature, and realistic standards of judgment are inappropriate. We might wonder to what extent the Western figures are designed to make the works more acceptable or intelligible to the Western reader. Probably they are just part of a natural way of communicating for a writer in the midst of acculturation, reflecting the ordinary Nigerian's deep interest in Western technology and selected Western customs.

For no assignable reason, these Westernizing figures are not nearly so conspicuous in Tutuola's next three novels. Repeated search locates only one in *Simbi and the Satyr of the Dark Jungle:* when Simbi falls down inside the hollow tree she makes a sort of bed of the "refuses," especially the "fluffy" ones; her bed is "just like a mattress." In *The Brave African Huntress* the followers of the monster Odara make a noise like "thousand of hooligans . . . following their cruel and merciless leader to some place where they were going to cause harm to several people." It sounds like a Western-style riot, or a lynching. In the Jungle of the Pigmies the Huntress climbs a tree and peeps out through the leaves "as when an offender peeped out from the small window of his cell." In this jungle, doves are likened to clocks; they cry "at five minutes interval as they were telling the other creatures the right time (clock)." When the Huntress fashions the skull of the "animal that died but his eyes still alive" into a headpiece, it seems to her just like a "cock" (cork) helmet. The Huntress finds a jungle fruit that is "as sweet as chocolate," and part of it is "just as ice cream." [41] In *Feather Woman of the Jungle* the pit in which the narrator and his "junior brother" bury their money is called their safe, a rare example of a Westernizing metaphor. The chief of the savage people who rides the narrator piggy-back in the cave presses "every part of his body" "as if he were a doctor." When he approaches the palace of the Queen of the River the narrator sees men lined up on both sides of the road "like policemen or soldiers"; we might suppose that Tutuola is reminded of the processions of imperial dignitaries in Nigeria. In Ede the narrator meets the God of Thunder, who makes rain by shaking a pebble-filled gourd shaped "like . . . bottle of beer." [42]

Tutuola's most effective syncretism involves his monsters: some of his ogres and ogresses are mechanized or technicalized. In *The Palm-Wine Drinkard* the king of the "field Creatures" is a sort of technological ogre, for "a hot steam was rushing out of his nose and mouth as a big boiler." One of Drinkard's most formidable opponents is Spirit of Prey, whose "eyes brought out a floodlight like mercury in color." The great white tree in which Faithful-Mother lives "was focusing" Drinkard and his wife "as if a photographer was focusing somebody," and when Drinkard and his wife run in terror, the animated tree cried out in a terrible voice "suddenly as if many persons talked into a big tank," and then with two large hands "made the sign of STOP," presumably like a traffic policeman.[43]

In *My Life in the Bush of Ghosts* the golden ghost, the "copperish" and the "silverish" ghost can cast their colored light on to the narrator, and the light cast by the silverish ghost "transparented every part of [his] body," apparently like a fluoroscope. In the dark underground room full of snakes in the ninth town of Ghosts, the chief snake, that was "acting as a director for the rest," vomited a kind of colored lights from his mouth, rather like colored stage lights.

The flash-eyed mother, a colossal stationary monstrosity that "filled the town as a vast round hill and that did not stand up or move to anywhere at all," has a characteristic even more fearsome than the millions of baby heads sounding like church bells—the eyes that flash fire to light firewood "like petrol or other inflammable spirit or gunpowder," to light her town "as electricity lights," or to execute her subjects, the short ghosts, "as fluffy things or rags." The flash-eyed mother wakes them up with a "terrible alarm which was in a hidden part of her body," something like a factory whistle. The Television-handed Ghostess, the three-foot creature covered with sores and maggots, as her name indicates has a television screen in her hand in which the wanderer in the Bush of Ghosts can see his "town, mother, brother, and all [his] playmates." [44]

The Satyr of the Dark Jungle has floodlight eyes which "illuminated to every part of that spot [where Simbi and her friend are standing] immediately he goggled both eyes." The "Super-Animal" of the *Brave African Huntress* also has illuminating eyes; indeed the illumination works even after the creature's death, which explains Tutuola's name for him, the "animal that died but his eyes still alive." The huntress makes a kind of helmet flashlight out of the creature's skull, and on two occasions uses the light to help her shoot down fleeing pigmies.[45]

One curious example of Tutuola's creativity would seem to involve syncretism, although it has never really been satisfactorily explained: the special designations for days of the week in *The Brave African*

Huntress. These rather intriguing epithets sound as though they referred to some body of African thought—"Day of Confusion Wednesday," "Day of New Creation which was Thursday," "Day of Trouble which was Friday," "Day of Three Resolutions Saturday," "Day of Immortality which was Sunday." [46] The epithets seem to have nothing to do with the traditional Yoruba naming of days, either by the names of the native four-day week or by reference to a market day in one of the towns (as "next *oja dugbe*" for "next market day at Dugbe"), or to a festival. Tutuola's name for Friday suggests the Christian associations with Good Friday; that for Sunday may simply refer to a prominent idea associated with the Christian Sabbath. But the other names are puzzling indeed. Apparently some non-Yoruba ideas, possibly some original notions, are being blended with traditional materials.

CHAPTER 5

The West Africans' Shame

W HEN Tutuola's romances were first published, educated West Africans, as we have already observed, seemed to be worried about certain social effects of his work. They professed to fear that his "immersion in the mythical past with its gods, ghosts, wars, sacrifices, and submerged terrors" set a bad example; they thought that such a preoccupation delayed progress.[1]

I *The Case against Tutuola as "Bad Example"*

Certainly it is true that Nigerians need pragmatic, not mythical, thought for their staggering tasks in social, political, and industrial organization. They have a desperate need for the best kind of progressive social thought, and backward-looking mystery-mongering would indeed be socially dangerous. But in their scramble for material progress Nigerians could lose the humane values of their old culture. As John Dewey, no great defender of backward methods of thought, says in *Reconstruction in Philosophy:*

> Surely there is no more significant question before the world than this question of the possibility and method of reconciliation of the attitudes of practical science and contemplative esthetic appreciation. Without the former, man will be the sport and victim of natural forces which he cannot use or control. Without the latter, mankind might become a race of economic monsters, restlessly driving hard bargains with nature and one another, bored with leisure or capable of putting it to use only in ostentatious display and extravagant dissipation.[2]

Such a warning seems peculiarly pertinent for "emerging" Africans, though perhaps American life itself speaks even more eloquently on the subject—if Nigerians will but observe. Does it really matter that Tutuola's ghost novels do not suggest ways to educate and hospitalize Nigerians and raise the Nigerian standard of living?

Surely his novels do show the spirit in which these high priority works should be achieved, and of course Nigerians will continue doing great quantities of technical or "useful" reading (Tutuola does himself).[3]

The West Africans' fear that fantastic, mythologizing romances like Tutuola's would hinder progress by encouraging mythological thinking is largely unfounded. Such a notion does not take sufficient account of the dynamic appeal of Western technology and its promise of a higher standard of health and comfort (and perhaps excitement). A more pressing danger is an indiscriminate lust for all kinds of Western technology, suitable and unsuitable, beneficial and harmful, and a kind of mad passion for Western clothes and recreations, even the tawdriest of them—all of this coupled with a curious kind of compensatory, hypertrophied propriety.

Besides, Tutuola's mythology is distinctly denatured; it is anything but pure Yoruba polytheism and animism. Tutuola is a Christian and not a nominal Christian either. Only in *Simbi* and *Feather Woman* are the specific religious beliefs and practices of the Yoruba clearly recognizable. As we noted earlier, Ulli Beier has suggested that it is Tutuola's uninformed Christian horror of the old gods that makes his monsters so conspicuous and so frightful. Tutuola has merely used some of the old religion and philosophy for his esthetic purposes. Although he has said that he "more than half-believes" his own tales,[4] we would probably do well to take this half-belief as the normal "belief" that a poet or non-realistic fiction writer feels for his work, or perhaps as the *nachschein* in the depths of Tutuola's mind left by the old beliefs and practices.

It is true that a few educated West Africans have gone back to some of the beliefs of the traditional cults, in what may prove a temporary nationalistic reaction to the religious arrogance, dogmatism, and ethnocentrism of Europeans. These neo-traditionalists apparently are not hostile to all of Western culture. As we shall see, some of the best Nigerian fiction is nostalgic about the old traditional life, but this nostalgia regrets the social forms and the integrative effects of the old cults rather than their view of nature or any religious belief that would be calculated to oppose progress. If West Africans should counter that even Christian mythology has in fact occasionally impeded the progress of rational scientific thought, we might answer that if it did so, it did not impede such progress any more than certain other attitudes, such as the Greek contempt for the kind of rational thought developed by the despised artisans, and we might add that all sorts of mythologies have resided in Western minds in separate compartments from the compartment of rational thought.

With political independence, cultural independence in Nigeria seems to be making gains. A passage from Chinua Achebe's novel *No Longer at Ease* seems to illustrate this slow growth toward cultural independence and ease:

They were eating pounded yams and *egusi* soup with their fingers. The second generation of educated Nigerians had gone back to eating pounded yams or *garri* with their fingers for the excellent reason that it tasted better that way. Also for the even better reason that they were not as scared as the first generation of being called uncivilized.[5]

Perhaps to admire Tutuola would be like eating *egusi* soup with the fingers. Even yet such admiration comes hard, because Nigerians still believe that Europeans and Americans have admired Tutuola for reasons humiliating to Nigerians. The worry about mythological thinking may be a rationalization of this false shame.

II *Western Writing on African Themes*

A good deal of the educated West Africans' antagonism toward Tutuola's work and their resentment of Western critics' praise of it may well be a result of their shame about the observances of the traditional religions, especially human sacrifice, the political atrocities of the old order, including slaving, and most important, the traditional belief in spirits, magic, and witchcraft. Of course this shame has been inculcated indirectly by Western education and directly by a host of travelers' and explorers' accounts of the old Africa and by missionary memoirs.

III *Is Africa Really Backward?*

Were we to take a brief but comprehensive view of the African situation—and the position of both Tutuola and his critics would seem to require that we do so—the analysis might run somewhat as follows. After considering the not always edifying English literature about Africa we can perhaps better understand the educated West Africans' hypersensitivity about mythological modes of thought and too much mention of the more bloodthirsty old African customs. We can easily imagine, and sympathize with, the mingled shame and disgust felt by educated West Africans when Westerners, with lofty complacency, gloat over the (often exaggerated) human sacrifices of old West Africa and the occasional ritual murder or atrocity committed by tribal and detribalized Africans of our day. Because Westerners have had power over West Africans and so have not heard as much criticism as the health of their souls requires, they have totally forgotten (deliberately or unconsciously?) the horrors of the West—the heads stuck on pikes at castle gates, the burnings of witches and heretics, the sacked cities, and the pogroms; and now the saturation bombings (killing and roasting thousands in one night), the napalm fire-bombing of simple peasants' huts on three continents, the gang wars (adult and juvenile), and the tender and merciful ministrations of H-bombs, machine guns, burp guns, bayonets, flame throwers, booby traps, and castor oil.

And, admittedly, educated West Africans with thin skins who worry about Tutuola's mythology are quite right about the monumental, willful, prejudice-serving ignorance of most Europeans and Americans about the new Africa, and their penchant for seizing upon the real and imagined shortcomings of Africans to preserve this gratifying ignorance. Probably most Westerners stereotype Africans as wild men in the bush, in spite of the spate of dependable scholarly studies, the helpful TV documentaries, and the more knowledgeable journalistic travel books. Too many Westerners fail to recognize the very considerable degree of Westernization that has taken place (the Mammy wagons, the Nigerian TV, the gas stations, etc.) and the widespread passionate desire for Western education, for industrialization. Their image of Africans entirely ignores all the dynamic desires driving Africans out of the bush and into some hitherto unimagined condition, some amalgam of Western technology and updated traditional politics, sociology, and religion.

Westerners, furthermore, are usually abysmally ignorant about the indigenous African cultures. Because these cultures have been less impressive in their technology than our own culture, we assume for them "primitive" social and political organizations, crude art forms, and naive philosophical and religious speculations, whereas actually, an unprejudiced study of African cultures might well give the reader the impression that the social and political organizations of the West are fragmentary, haphazard, and chaotic as compared to traditional African organizations. For instance, the novels of Chinua Achebe give a credible picture of the wholesomeness and fulfilling quality of the traditional Ibo culture. Where the Africans have produced something fine and "civilized," like the Benin bronzes, Westerners have until recently explained away African merit by positing fanciful alien originators. Or if the merit is unmistakable and no alien influences are conceivable, even to prejudice, then the art form is downgraded as not particularly important—for instance, African dancing. Some African artistic achievements we are entirely ignorant of. Probably we will one day cite African music as a cultural triumph.

Western ridicule is a sword that has two edges. If we gloat over the Africans' trouble governing themselves, we may be forgetting that South and Central Americans—even Frenchmen—have the same trouble. If we sneer because Africans have never invented a script for writing, we may be forgetting that we owe our own script not to Europeans but to the presumably brown Phoenicians. Westerners who could not re-invent the most simple element of our complex technology—say the lever—gibe at Africans for the simple technology of their traditional cultures.[6]

It is conceivably true that Tutuola's wildly imaginative fiction, in sixth-grade grammar and full of mistakes and eccentric freedoms, could activate such brutal ignorance and prejudice and seem to nullify the painstaking attempts of Nigerian intellectuals to teach the Westerners better. And it is frustrating to see one's laborious educational efforts just knocked on the head! We may hope, however, that this touchiness of the West Africans will one day be cured by their satisfying themselves on the true reasons for the backwardness of Africa in the modern age, reasons which will not be humiliating.

Still, before anyone tries to explain the backwardness he must define it accurately. The native African economic systems and the native technologies, modes of production and exchange, medical science, and the other sciences are obviously far behind those of the West. In the non-technical, non-economic areas, on the other hand, the situation is not nearly so clear; African family systems, forms of marriage, ethical and religious principles, political organizations, art, music, and dancing are not nearly so obviously backward, or not so at all. The open-minded Westerner cannot help admiring the warmth of kinship feeling in Africans and their respect for the aged; he can respect African religions and African religious devotion (wincing at the memories of the ignorant slanders of the missionaries on this subject); perhaps he can even feel some envy of the close integration of societies achieved by the social and political systems of the various African peoples.

The art of Africans is of course anything but inferior. The ceremonial masks, the ivory carvings, the figurines, the statues in wood, brass, and bronze of the Congo, the Guinea Coast, and the Western Sudan suggest, if anything, a superiority in the plastic arts for certain parts of Africa. Probably the ornamentation of household articles and other utensils is superior. Moreover, it is likely that African music, when it is better known, in all its regional varieties, will make contributions to Western music as important as the well-known African contribution of Jazz. And one might well imagine that Africa leads the rest of the world in the art of the dance.[7]

But how are we to account for the backwardness in the technical matters of science and economics, if not by the simple theory of the innate inferiority of the African, as the racists would have it? Probably we should search for the causes in the physical environment of what Peter Ritner calls the "pauper continent." Africa's soils are the poorest in the world, and continually growing worse. Few of her rivers are navigable from their estuaries. Good harbors are scarce. The harborless coasts and the unnavigable rivers, together with the dense mangrove forests of the coasts, discouraged European contacts from the sea. The Sahara was a barrier to Europeans (though not to North Africans) in the north. The climate in much of the continent is ferocious; even nowadays expatriate professionals and businessmen working in West Africa cannot function properly without trips home every two years or so. The diseases which torment Africans are simply nightmarish horrors. Any reader who is inclined to feel superior to Africans should read George Kimble's account of the major diseases of tropical Africa, which include malaria, sleeping sickness, bilharziasis, leprosy, tuberculosis, hookworm, filiariasis (including elephantiasis), pellagra, kwashiorkor, ascariasis, yaws, amoebic and bacillary dysentery, pneumonia, ulcers, pneumonic, bubonic, and septicemic plague, typhus, yellow fever, relapsing fevers, smallpox, and meningitis. Considering the seriousness of these diseases and the very high incidence of them, we may wonder how Africans have been able to achieve anything at all.[8] Immigrants from southern Europe suffering from similar depressing environments have showed their worth by prospering in the United States. No doubt the enforced immigrants from Africa would similarly have disabused us of any notion of their inferiority had we not enslaved them, made them helots, brainwashed them into believing in their own inferiority!

Besides the terrible burdens of the "pauper continent," the Africans have suffered from a very great social disorder. Perhaps educated Africans have exaggerated the retarding effect of slavery on African cultures and downgraded the Africans' own share of guilt in this great crime against humanity, but it would seem obvious that the slave trade did sustain and exacerbate social disorganization and warfare, which were certainly not helpful to African cultures, and African slavery was much encouraged by the presence of alien slavers on the two coasts.[9]

IV *Tutuola and His Contemporaries*

By now we have a fairly large body of West African fiction to compare with Tutuola's. And it is obvious that Tutuola is not the only writer to face the problem of taking up some sort of position toward the old Africa, the pristine, so-called (and improperly called) pagan Africa, with its mythological thinking. Should the writer consider this past a kind of golden age spoiled by the white intruders, or a nightmare from which he is trying to awake, or what? His society being in a phase of conspicuous and rapid change under Western influence, he cannot escape judging the African whence and the Westernized whither of such change. Amos Tutuola has not been the least bit embarrassed by the difficulty. He has accepted the old way of life, including some of the less creditable elements like human sacrifice, and perhaps even exaggerated the old-African preoccupation with spirits, gods, and the revered ancestors. Tutuola has conveyed this rather feverish, hag-ridden vision of old Africa in a kind of dream-like phantasmagoria.

But perhaps it is misleading to say that Tutuola accepts the traditional way of life; he simply renders it—or as some Nigerian nationalists would say, renders a nightmarish distortion of it—with emphasis on the traditional African's preoccupation with malevolent spirits and magical transformations. And yet at the same time, Tutuola, a great artist of the unconscious sort, manages to be hopeful and excited about Western instruments, customs, and institutions, and his syncretism or grafting of Western ways and gear into Yoruba folk myths (especially in the episodes involving the Super Lady and the Methodist Church of the Bush of Ghosts) is one of the most interesting aspects of his art. Surely, Tutuola's is one reasonable way, though of course not the only reasonable way, of relating to the African past. The virtues of his folk heroes still have some relevance for our dreams at least, and possibly for our unconscious. At any rate, Tutuola is able to admit the worst in the old ways without apology and the best (or parts of it) in the new ways without excessive deference to the Westerners.

The African writer may, like T. M. Aluko in his humorous novel, *One Man, One Wife* (1959), light-heartedly reject and ridicule the traditional life. This attitude is now uncommon: Nigerian intellectuals were outraged by Aluko's merriment over the Yoruba worship of the smallpox god, the corrupt agents of the Oba or King, and the senile chief and his feckless councilors. Note these serious and inept lines of Denis Osadebey's, written about a dozen years ago, illustrating an earlier attitude rather like Aluko's:

> My simple fathers
> In childlike faith
>   believed all things;
> It cost them much
> And their offspring lost a lot;
> They questioned not the
>   lies of magic
> And fetish seemed
>   to have some logic.[10]

Or the wandering-between-two-worlds African writer may, like Cyprian Ekwensi in his well-known novel *Jagua Nana* (1961), show much more interest in the pleasures and satisfactions of Westernized life—such things as the "jaguar" courtesan's fine clothes and her free loving, the Tropicana Club (a "sex market"), girl gas station attendants in space suits, and high-powered modern politicking—than in the rather dimly conceived traditional life, as illustrated in a visit to Nana's home village and her boy friend's home village.

Or the African writer may, like Chinua Achebe in his fine novel *Things Fall Apart* (1958), look back with nostalgia toward the old, contented, orderly, sensible, integrated traditional life, describing with care such things as the Ibo oracle, the marriage customs, the funeral customs, the yam festival, and the *egwugwu* masquerade, presenting the advent of the whites with their ignorant justice and fanatical religion as an almost unmitigated disaster for Iboland. Perhaps the reader is familiar with the most distinguished writer in this school of African nostalgia, the French-speaking poet Léopold Sédar Senghor, whose verse is full of memories of the old African life: of "ancestors," "Gambia or Saloum," "dancers," "the smoky hut," "the Kuskos ball smoking out of the fire," and the "black and red masks," and complaints about "the white hands that loaded the guns that destroyed the kingdoms" and "the world that has died of machines and cannons," the world of "No mother's breasts, but only nylon legs." [11]

V *Final Basis of Judgment*

In spite of the literary success and productivity of Senghor's and Achebe's nostalgic stance toward the traditional African past, we may suspect that there is more of an artistic future for Tutuola's cheerful forward-looking attitude. Tutuola seems to discriminate more carefully among Western customs and gear than Ekwensi does, and Tutuola's mythologizing is surely a perfectly valid literary approach.

In any discussion of Tutuola's works, critics need to keep reminding themselves that they must establish the purely literary values of the works and not muddle the critical issue by concentrating upon all kinds of sociological and paraliterary concerns. Whether the Nigerians were in the past or are now in the present barbarous; whether the Tutuola romances do or do not encourage mythological thinking among West Africans and contempt for Nigerians among Europeans; whether Nigerian novels should be based on folk tales or follow the traditions of the European realistic novel; whether they should be written in English or in the various vernaculars; whether Nigerian literature should approve or disapprove of the African past —perhaps even whether Nigerian literature should be addressed to Nigerians or to Europeans and Americans—this heap of issues should be kept in abeyance until we read all the romances and judge them as examples of their genre—the fantastic romance. What is their literary success? Are the romances good in their kind, or not? Afterwards, the other issues may exercise the critics' ingenuity and their critical acumen; the issues are important, but what critics think about them should not sway their judgment on purely literary values.

CHAPTER 6

The Language of the Romances

IT has not been feasible to begin this study by a consideration of
Tutuola's language, but the first thing about his work to strike
the reader—and it strikes hard—is his language. It is probably altogether unique in the history of our literature. Vigorous and magnificently assured, it is wildly "incorrect," a kind of grand literary
defiance of all the English-teaching schoolmarms of the world. This
writer has heard one of the country's most distinguished linguists
fulminate about Tutuola's grammatical atrocities. But unlike grammarians (even descriptive grammarians), literary critics, especially
connoisseurs of style, usually find Tutuola's language supple, forceful, graphic, and straightforward. Indeed Tutuola's style is a great
style—in a non-standard species of English. The following random
sample will demonstrate how much power Tutuola gets into his
language, in spite of the strange diction and the violations of idiom
(and perhaps sometimes *because of* the strangeness and the violations):

As I was carrying him along the road, he was trying all his efforts to
escape or to kill me, but I did not give him a chance to do that. When I
had travelled about eight hours, then I reached the town and went straight
to the old man's house who told me to go and bring Death from his house.
When I reached the old man's house, he was inside his room, then I called
him and told him that I had brought Death that he told me to go and
bring. But immediately he heard from me that I had brought Death and
when he saw him on my head, he was greatly terrified and raised alarm
that he thought nobody could go and bring Death from his house, then
he told me to carry him (Death) back to his house at once, and he (old
man) hastily went back to his room and started to close all his doors and
windows, but before he could close two or three of his windows, I threw
down Death before his door and at the same time that I threw him down,
the net cut into pieces and Death found his way out.[1]

I *Varying Opinions*

Tutuola's vigorous English, however we may describe it, is most certainly not the Queen's English. Critics have exercised their ingenuity trying to characterize it. Paul Bohannon, writing in the *Listener* of May 13, 1954, has called it a combination of schoolboy English, officialese, and West African pidgin. It is true that there is in Tutuola's English a certain headlong forthrightness, an assured naïveté, that might suggest a certain kind of schoolboy's writing, though many schoolboys are painfully self-conscious and stilted in their writing, and some of Tutuola's vocabulary is rather beyond the range of a schoolboy. It is also true that occasionally a heaviness of vocabulary, a lumbering clumsiness of the syntax, does remind us of the jargon of government offices. However, to call Tutuola's English partly pidgin is rather misleading. His English, though furiously non-standard, is distinctly English in vocabulary and grammar: pidgin English is practically a separate language with its own grammar. A comparison between a random sample of Tutuola's English and a representation of pidgin from Gabriel Okara's story "The Crooks" in *Black Orpheus* will give some notion of the difference:

> Tutuola: His both feet were very long and thick
> as a pillar of a house, but no shoes
> would size his feet in this world.
>
> Pidgin: I tell dem say I get big 'tranger so
> they come salute you. All be big people.
> Na we dey sell motor for dis town.[2]

Beyond the instances of such pidgin expressions as "too much," there is not a great deal of pidgin in Tutuola's exotic English. Geoffrey Parrinder, lecturer at the University of Ibadan, simply calls it "English as it is spoken in West Africa." [3]

In his interviews of Amos Tutuola in *West Africa*, "A Nigerian Correspondent" notes that Tutuola's "spoken and written English are identical," though his speech does not reflect the vivid imagination shown in his writing, and the interviewer offers the suggestion that Tutuola in his writing "merely translates in a literal fashion from the Yoruba in which all the old legends are verbally told." [4] A Nigerian exchange teacher of the writer's acquaintance, possibly not wishing to offend an admirer of Tutuola's work by too severe a stricture, mildly observed that Tutuola's language is about what one would expect from an intelligent West African who had not been able to attend a secondary school. Professor Martin Banham, at the time lecturer at the University of Ibadan, has told the writer that Tutuola's English seems to him a "broken English" showing the effects of his straining to write literate, formal English (though Banham readily admitted that such an effort on the part of college freshmen all too often produced a kind of English as unlike Tutuola's as one could well imagine—jargonish, pretentious, and dead). Professor Banham then called Tutuola's English "junior clerk English," which is probably the most helpful designation mentioned so far, especially if we emend the designation slightly to read "inspired junior clerk English."

One quality not mentioned by the critics but noticeable to any reader who immerses himself in Tutuola's work and certainly worth mentioning is the stability, the self-consistency, the inevitableness of the language. The quality is not easy to describe, but we might say that when we have read a number of Tutuola's works, we catch ourselves reading conventional English as though it were Tutuolese, very much as when we return from abroad we read English signs as though they were in the foreign language we have recently been living with. Perhaps this is just a way of saying that Tutuola's English is not, like the clumsy freshman themes, merely ineptitude, but a real language with power. But more on that issue later.

II *Oral Quality*

There is considerable critical agreement on one aspect of Tutuola's English: its oral quality. Gerald Moore, of the University of Sussex, one of the most perceptive critics of Tutuola, in taking notice of this oral quality has spoken of the "warm human voice" speaking in his style. Moore reports that, though the experience of having Tutuola read his stories over the Nigerian radio was not a success because of his shyness, when others read the stories they were an "instant success." V. S. Pritchett has praised Tutuola's "loose, talking prose," and notes the "soft, amazed voice" that narrates the first novel.[5]

Mr. S. Akanji Dawada, principal of a teachers' college in Lagos, had a spirited discussion with the writer in a series of literary coffee breaks, on Tutuola's qualities. Partly moved by the traditional African courtesy (perhaps wholly so moved), Mr. Dawada finally admitted that he had probably been blind to some of Tutuola's positive merits, but he could not honestly say that he saw Tutuola's *con brio* exuberance. Perhaps he was—understandably—too upset about Tutuola's "crudities" and the misconceptions they would give rise to, to observe the vitality. Or perhaps we need to be native to the language to understand the vigor of his nonstandard dialect.

III *Style*

But it is not nearly as important to place Tutuola's English in the proper social and usage level as it is to recognize its power and grace. Gerald Moore quite correctly calls Tutuola "one of the two supreme stylists among living African prose writers" (the other is the French-speaking novelist Camara Laye). The anthropologist John V. Murra has called Tutuola's English a "terse, graphic, and personal" kind of "young English." Pritchett suggests some of its compelling power by saying that "Tutuola's voice is like the beginning of man on earth, man emerging, wounded and growing. . . ." [6]

When we are reading Tutuola we are very likely to interrupt the wife's reading of the *New Yorker* with expressions of great pleasure and read out to her such things as "I did not satisfy with it. . . . This lady refused totally to marry that man. . . . I was shaking together with my voice. . . . Beat him greedily. . . . Bad-bye function. . . . She never acrossed such a wonderful orchestra. . . . Simbi said whisperly. . . . I had leaked out the secret. . . . I fed up to be alive any more." [7]

IV *Representative Samples*

But it is time to let the reader observe for himself the clarity, directness, vigor, and felicity of Tutuola's language, as illustrated in several extended extracts. The description of the flash-eyed mother is fairly representative:

This "flash-eyed mother" sat on the ground in the centre of town permanently. She did not stand up or move to anywhere at all, she was all the time beaten there by both rain and sun, both day and night. There was no single house built in this town as she alone filled the town as a round vast hill, it was hard for the real inhabitants to move about or sleep in the town. This town is about six miles in circumference, it was as clean as a football field. All these short ghosts were just exactly a year and an half old babies, but very strong as iron and clever while doing everything, all of them had no other work more than to be killing the bush animals with short guns like pistols . . . .

The battle boast of the Satyr of the Dark Jungle, one of many such heroic bombastic outbursts, is typical:

When they were unable to reply to all his questions, then he started to explain to them his terrible deeds. "Certainly you have put yourselves into the mouth of 'death'! You have climbed the tree above its leaves! You see me coming and you too are coming to me instead to run away for your lives!

By the way, have you not been told of my terrible deeds? And that I have killed and eaten so many persons, etc. who were even bold more than you do?

Here is a representative portrait of an ogre in *The Brave African Huntress:*

His navel was big that it could contain more than four gallons of water. It swelled out from his belly to a distance of about five feet. In respect of this fearful navel he was not wearing other cloth on his body except a big apron. Whenever he was walking very hastily along, this navel would be shaking and sounding heavily as when the water was shaking in a large tube and it appeared on his belly as if a very large bowl covered the belly.

Our last specimen, from *Feather Woman of the Jungle,* is an "action shot" of the confusion when the second magic box from under the water produced not food, but insects:

But uncountable of bees, wasps and all kinds of the stinging insects rushed out from it instead of food and drinks. Without hesitation, those insects started to sting all of us. Within a few minutes many people were stung to death, that place was disordered at the same time. Everyone was running skelter helter for his or her life. And at last, as the king was running away for his life, the crown fell off from his head but he was unable to wait and take it back.[8]

Surely the reader should agree with Ulli Beier, a very knowledgeable connoisseur of the West African arts and cultures, that Tutuola's very lack of education has given him "an innocent approach to the English language that allows him to distort it to suit his own purposes. . . ." Unfortunately, educated Nigerians cannot seem to appreciate the stylistic vitality produced by the distortions.

Although much of the distress of educated West Africans occasioned by Tutuola's English is due to their fear that it will suggest to English-speaking readers that Nigerians cannot write standard English, and to their rather prissy standards of style and diction, we must admit that Tutuola's grammar, vocabulary, and typography are sufficiently startling; they are stumbling blocks to proper appreciation of Tutuola's work. Tutuola's linguistic practices will repay a closer, more detailed study. Somewhat arbitrarily, we will start with his grammar and syntax, and then consider his vocabulary and his typography.

V *Grammar and Syntax*

Tutuola's grammar is at least as exotic as his vocabulary. He shows more than Elizabethan boldness, which makes for a certain vigor as he shifts parts of speech: *would jealous him more than that, transparented every part of my body, took out the rest meat* ("rest of the meat," a very common form in Tutuola), *does not severe enough, did not aware, never acrossed such an orchestra, pain of the beats, was leaning more* (getting thinner), *he was a talkative, a great funny to us* (like our colloquial "make a funny"), *they naked themselves, as many as would sufficient for us.* Tutuola has a number of adverbs, usually with verbs of saying or asking, that are new in form or the way they are used: *looking at each of them surprisingly, perplexly asked, asked painfully, said whisperly, laughing at us funningly, fixed its eyes staringly.* There are several adjectives with elegant new adverbial suffixes: *a really man* (much more real than a "real man" somehow), *a slightly air* (on a bugle). Tutuola's new conjunctions, which are fairly frequent, probably contribute the officialese component of his style: he often uses *that which* for *that* or *which* and *that why* for our *why* and *that what* for *what;* for the *that* of broad reference, referring to a previous statement, he uses *like that: Sell me? No, you cannot do that . . . Having said like that.*[9]

In Tutuola's English queer things happen to verbs. To the grammarian the most conspicuous feature of his verb management would probably be his extensive use of the progressive forms, giving a sharp immediacy to much of the violent action: *he was still looking at me as he was running away, this Satyr was looking at them with these eyes, it was so I was killing them.* The ordinary reader might notice more readily—and be disconcerted by—frequent reversals in voice, active forms for passive and passive forms for active: *did not satisfy with it, who deputed for us at home, I free from all these punishments, all his efforts were failed, having disappointed by the gods, have they caught by my trap, as he was snivelled, camels were commonly seeing everywhere.*[10]

In syntax or sentence structure any reader would notice the tautologies, syncopations, sentence fragments, and strange idioms. The tautologies are often rather attractive, often sharpen the meaning:

I had no other work more than to drink palm-wine, she had no other sons more than both of us, his eyes were shedding tears repeatedly, thinking in mind (common), *eating together with witches, breathe in and out* (also common).[11] The syncopations make for a kind of bold economy of language which is pleasant: *the king gave one of them a sharp stick to stab us, perhaps we might talk* (the conjunction expressing purpose or result is suppressed), *the king told attendants to wash and dress us, etc. which meant to enjoy our last life* ("that we should" suppressed), *if the rest heard the sound of my gun might rush out to kill me* (again the subject in the subordinate clause is missing; "they" is suppressed).[12]

The strange idioms are of course legion; they are hardly ever obscure, and sometimes they are rather interesting. These samples will show that the idioms are not particularly formidable to the careful reader: *trying all his efforts, began to feel to go, became to the size of a baby, shot my gun . . . to him, it was so I was throwing this key up* (common form in Tutuola), *to scold at us, shone to our eyes.*[13] Tutuola's comparatives and superlatives in his occasional little gnomic summaries of perilous situations might give trouble until the reader puzzles out his conventions, which are slightly different from those of standard English: *harder to stay in the bag and hardest to come out* might be translated into standard English as "terribly hard to stay in the bag and incredibly hard to come out."[14]

As for the fragments, we might simply observe that they are most frequent in the last three romances, that they are *not* the sort justified in the more liberal manuals of rhetoric—answers to questions, transitional expressions, and so on—and that they ought not to bother anyone unduly unless he is a purist: *But as we were just freed from that wild animals, and we were still descending the mountain. There we heard a horrible shout from the top of the mountain.* (Occasionally in Tutuolese, as in this sentence fragment, *that* seems to operate as a plural.)[15]

We will conclude this examination of Tutuola's linguistic offenses by mentioning his unconventional use of percentages and *etc.*—in standard English used only in mathematical and statistical contexts —and his frequent parentheses, especially in the first novel, to keep his pronoun references straight: *about ninety per cent of them* (the cruel "unknown creatures") *also burnt with the houses, it would be bad for me and the people, etc. of my village, when the debit-collector for the £1 which he* (borrower) *had borrowed from his friend.* The percentages and *etc.* may be considered colloquial locutions in a commercial civilization, matching such obvious colloquial forms as *invitees, full up with water,* and (beautifully adapted!) *fed up to be alive any more.*[16]

Tutuola's innocent manhandling of our language gives results that are extremely interesting for language study; they suggest the malleability of the language, the possibilities in the language for creative expansion and development, for freshness, and for the assimilation of alien ideas.

VI *Vocabulary*

Of course many of Tutuola's inventions are items of vocabulary. Some of these are simply fresh words for ideas expressed by the regular vocabulary, like *refused totally, alives or deads,* or *suspect us* (give away our position) *to the phoenix,* but usually the new words bear an increment of new meaning, as in *longing to sleep heavily* (suggests the persistent burden of sleepiness), *produce out anything* (emphasizing the emergence of the products), *burglary wars* (real candor on foreign affairs!), *dead luck, sweet and lofty smell, bad-bye function* (sad farewell party), *decline from her wish* (indicating the sliding away from a resolution), *they were scrambling me very greedily* (roughing her up terribly), *redundant husband* (a pungent comment on bad domestic relations).[17]

Often Tutuola's words are used in a slightly different context from the standard one, or they carry a meaning associated with the meaning of the standard word: *lavish all the drinks* (drink heavily), *risible man* (comedian), *she was the only issue of her mother, disallowed me from seeing, noxious creatures, speak out the matter to that hole, hastily held his big goitre, cut away my left foot unexpectedly, the whole secrets, entirely tired, beat me to their satisfaction* (quite common in Tutuola), *abundant of them had returned, obstructing that ostrich with her hands, incited them* (dogs) *to the men, continued to hurtle to everywhere.* Sometimes a very small change is involved: *saw his havocs, prove out* (check out and prove thoroughly), *amputy* for the foreign-sounding *amputee, hurthing here and there* (hurtling?).[18]

VII *Typography*

A good deal of the impression of oddness conveyed by Tutuola's language is produced by his typographical eccentricities. Probably most conspicuous of these eccentricities is his special uses of capitals and quotation marks. In *Drinkard* the text is divided at short intervals by section headings, sometimes with all-capitals, sometimes with all-capitals and quotation marks: "DO NOT FOLLOW UNKNOWN MAN'S BEAUTY"; ON OUR WAY TO THE UNRETURNABLE-HEAVEN'S TOWN. *My Life in the Bush of Ghosts* and the other romances have conventional chapter headings, but *Simbi* has a few section headings, with all-capitals: BAKO, THE TERRIBLE SIAMESE TWIN; THE PUNISHMENT OF SIMBI IN THE TOWN OF THE MULTICOLOURED PEOPLE.[19]

Sometimes Tutuola seems to be indicating proper names with the use of quotation marks (reinforcing the capitals, as it were): "Exhibition of Smells," "Bush of Ghosts," "Invisible Missive Magnetic Juju," "Day of New Creation," "The Day of Trouble," "The Day of Immortality," "Shakabullah" gun. The name for the juju device is almost like a trade name; the names for days are like our names for holidays and holy days. Sometimes he further emphasizes the proper name quality by all-capitals, as in "GIVE AND TAKE," the name of a magical worker (the name is merely capitalized on the next page), "THE METHODIST CHURCH OF THE BUSH OF GHOSTS," "SECRET SOCIETY OF GHOSTS."[20] In *Drinkard* the names of Song, Drum, and Dance are treated three ways, with capitalization, with all-capitals, and with all-capitals and quotation marks. Strange as it seems, Tutuola apparently uses quotation marks, with *lower case,* to indicate a proper name: "odara" is surely a proper name, and "obstacle" looks like one: "After I killed 'obstacle' I travelled in this jungle. . . . " Occasionally he uses all-capitals to emphasize a word—with rather startling effect; for instance, COWRIES and (with quotes) "POOR." At other times he seems to employ quotation marks to indicate that he is using a word in a special sense, but it is often hard to be sure: "He was a beautiful 'complete' gentleman . . ."; ". . . before we reached the 'mixed' town . . ."; "This front tree was a 'Sign' for me and it was on that day I called it—THE 'FUTURE SIGN.' " The last example is rather baffling. The whole sentence is quoted in the original, at the end of his description of his entering into the Bush of Ghosts; the double quotation marks simply serve as emphasis, apparently. The single quotation marks around *Sign* indicate perhaps use of a Western object in an African setting, with the capital for emphasis. The words in all-capitals and single quotation marks seem to constitute a proper noun.[21]

In the first two romances, Tutuola's use—rather inconsistent use—of mathematical signs and arabic figures for simple numbers gives the impression of great informality, or crudity, depending on tastes: "for that 7 days," "spent 15 days," "these 9 terrible creatures were short or 3 feet high," "increased by 60 per-cent," "which is the 8th town of ghosts" (all the numbered ghost towns are treated thus), "and it was 90 x 70 ft." Tutuola's treatment of numbers is not consistent: we find the more conventional usage too, as in, "about five minutes that they were looking at us." The following passage mixes conventional practice and bold innovation: "the attendance showed fifty old, thirty-eight young and forty-five child ghosts respectively who attended and all = 133." [22]

Tutuola's practice of using hyphens where they would normally not be used also makes his prose typographically distinctive. This hyphenation is most prominent in the first two romances; some of these forms are rather curious: "Wraith-Island," "Unreturnable-Heaven's town," "Faithful-Mother," "Faithful-Hands" (sometimes with quotes), "Red-people," "Red-smaller-tree," "Red-tree," "Red-king," "Red-leaves," etc., "River-ghosts," "Nameless-town," "Hope-less-town." Curiously, the one name that we would most expect to see hyphenated is written open: Super Lady.[23]

As conspicuous as the hyphens of the first two romances are the italics of *The Feather Woman of the Jungle*. Tutuola uses italics for a number of special purposes. The chapter titles are in italics; the titles under the chapter titles, indicating the number of the "entertainment," are in roman type; and the titles in the third bank, indicating the number of the journey, are in italics and in parentheses. The effect of the contrasting types, and of the practice in capitalization is illustrated by the first regular chapter heading:

The Witch of the Jungle
The entertainment of the first night
(*My first Journey*)[24]

Note the lower-case title of the second line, the mixed capitals and lower case of the third line. For a running chapter title the second-line title is used, italicized, and again with only the first word capitalized. We might add that one of the chapter headings has a particularly overpowering top line; and the use of selected capitals and italics helps to make it somehow strangely impressive:

The Foot Marks of the First White Men who had travelled from Heaven to the World were seen on the Rock in Ife Town. And we visited the Wells from which the Sun and Moon are rising into the Sky and we met the God of Thunder and his Wife in Ede Town.[25]

This is a kind of typographical poetry, and suggests that our conventionality about typography exacts a cost in missed power.

In *The Brave African Huntress* the curious and rather cryptic epigraphs under most of the chapter titles are in italics, which may support the oracular effect of these strange medleys of topics and statements. This epigraph would be representative:

The big gun that stops the voices of the soldiers
Animals are surplus in the town in which the people
have no teeth (Note absence of periods and manner of runover).

In this romance what seem to be folk sayings are italicized. On one occasion an italicized topic, sentence, and sentence fragment are used as a section heading in this romance, and although it is the only such use of italics here or elsewhere in the romances, it is sufficiently striking:

The thief who steals bugle. Where is he going to blow it? In this world of the white men or in heaven?

The gossiping remarks of the talking bugle are italicized and quoted.[26] In short, Tutuola uses his typographical resources with the same freedom and boldness as he does other elements of language.

VIII *Editorial Treatment of Tutuola's Language*

Obviously Tutuola's English presents editors with formidable problems. Generally speaking, Faber and Faber have kept the "clarification of the text" to a minimum, and less of this sort of "clarification" has been done in the last four novels.[27] A fairly close examination of the "page from the author's MS. showing the publisher's corrections" helpfully provided on page 24 of *The Palm-Wine Drinkard* will bring to the fore some of the problems involved. Of the dozen or so "corrections" on the page (it is not always clear which changes are the editor's), two deal with misspellings: *atal* for *at all* and *where-ever* for *wherever*. We might suppose that there would be no argument about these changes, though it may be worth mentioning that Tutuola's spelling of *at all* is phonetically accurate in its unemphatic position, and that its location in the sentence is as nonstandard as the spelling: "I could not blame the lady for following the Skull as a complete gentleman to his house at all." A possibly nonstandard verb form is regularized: "after I had drank [drunk] it all." Perhaps there might be some question about this change; we would need to know if *drank* or a free option *drank/drunk* occurs in Nigerian vernacular English; if the vernacular allows *drank* probably it should be used here. A possibly superfluous comma is removed in "Because if I were a lady, no doubt [,] I would follow him to wherever he would go." Perhaps this change is defensible, but then why don't we have the same short of change in a situation further down in the same sentence: "because if this gentleman go to the battle field, surely, [no change] enemy would not kill him. . . ."

The rest of the changes tinker up Tutuola's English a little closer to standard English. In referring to the beginning of detective Drinkard's work in the case of the lady and her skull husband, Tutuola writes thus (with editorial changes indicated in parentheses): "And when it was early in the morning, I sent for forty kegs of palm-wine, after I had drank (drunk) it all, then (marked out, apparently by the editor) I started to investigate where about the lady (whereabouts was the lady)." The *then* is probably tautological after the preceding *when* and *after*, but the time relations are sharper with it in. The other change is very interesting: apparently Tutuola had used a kind of elliptical verbless clause, which is perfectly clear, though certainly strange to our ears. Changing Tutuola's adverbs to a noun and adding *was,* besides being an extensive change, makes a rather nonstandard improvement; perhaps "investigate the lady's whereabouts" is a possibility, but the more we tinker the better the original expression looks.

In the passage describing the great beauty of the skull in his form with rented body parts, Tutuola writes thus (again, with changes indicated in parentheses):

And still as I was a man, I would jealous him more than that, because if this gentleman go (went) to the battle field, surely, enemy would not kill him or capture him and if bombers see (saw) him in a town which was to be bombed, they would not throw bombs on his presence, and if they threw (did throw) it, the bomb itself would not explode, until this gentleman would leave this town, because of his beauty.[28]

Perhaps readers will disagree about the propriety of touching up the simplicity of Tutuola's verbs here. And can we justify changing the verbs if we are going to leave "jealous him more than that," "enemy (rather than *the* enemy or *an* enemy) would not kill him," and "throw bombs on his presence"? And should the oddly placed "because of his beauty" dangle at the end? It does have a rather special effect there, as a kind of emphatic, summarizing coda. And the bad reference "bombs . . . it"?

Occasionally the editing of *The Palm-Wine Drinkard* and of *My Life in the Bush* is quite laissez-faire. The headings in the text of *The Palm-Wine Drinkard*—they are too close together to be called chapter headings—are sometimes in quotation marks, sometimes not. They are set up in all-capitals. Such a heading with quotation marks and all-capitals appears in the facsimile on page 24. In *My Life in the Bush of Ghosts* headings are spaced through the text like chapter headings; they are in the usual form, without quotation marks or all-capitals. Occasionally we see an important word capitalized that we would expect to see in lower case: "I become an Aggressor for Ghosts." In both novels Tutuola's inexplicable, apparently pointless (and inconsistent) use of quotation marks around some proper and common nouns is left alone: "When 'Drum' started to beat himself . . . ," "All the members of this church were 'evil-doers.'" "They sang the song of evils' with evils' melodious tune, then 'Judas' closed the service." [29]

The editing of the last four novels, even less strict than that of the first two, raises questions of editorial responsibility in the editing of nonconventional books. A reviewer in *Black Orpheus* signing himself "Akanji" and describing himself as a "detribalised Yoruba" has strongly protested Faber and Faber's practice of leaving uncorrected some of Tutuola's spelling errors in *The Brave African Huntress*. After giving the publishers credit for not wanting to "tamper with" Tutuola's "fresh West African idiom," he makes a great fuss over the uncorrected errors:

But it is rather unfair on the part of the publishers to leave even spelling mistakes uncorrected. Tutuola's language will lose none of its poetry, his style will not lose character if he is told that "gourd" is not spelled "guord." It is mere sensationalism on the part of the publishers not to correct a mistake like the following: "I thank you all for the worm affection you have on me." The publishers are in this case no longer interested to preserve Tutuola's originality; they are inviting the readers to have a good laugh at his expense. I wonder whether the publishers realise how much harm they do to Tutuola's reputation in West Africa through this kind of thing. There has been a great deal of opposition to Tutuola on the part of young West Africans. They suspect that his success in Europe is not based on literary merits but on his curiosity value. They feel that Europeans merely laugh at the "funny" language and "semi-literate" style of Tutuola.[30]

Well, discounting the imputed sensationalism and the alleged desire to raise a laugh against Tutuola, which this writer believes are simply not so, and noticing and deploring the hypersensitivity of the young West Africans, we may well agree with "Akanji" about the editorial impropriety of letting the misspellings stand. (Incidentally, we may suppose the publishers cried *peccavi* about the spelling of "gourd," for in *Feather Woman of the Jungle* "gourd" is spelled correctly.) We might also decide that the complaint of "Akanji" would apply to a number of other editorial decisions, especially in *Feather Woman of the Jungle*. Is there any point in having "believes" instead of "beliefs" or "savely" for "safely"? Though they may hint interestingly of the West African pronunciation of English, are "forg" or "deem light" for "fog" and "dim light" entirely justified? Don't these variations have a slightly ridiculous connotation about them, suggest the speech of foreigners? Again, "Dump" for "dumb" may also suggest pronunciation, in the unvoicing of the voiced consonant, but the misspelling should go: "The pain is that you will pretend to be dump for the period of two years." The word has too heavy a load of unsuitable connotations. It is interesting to note that another version of this episode printed as a short story in *Présence Africaine* has "dumb" spelled correctly.[31]

But to be fair to Faber and Faber we must continually remind ourselves how generally felicitous the hands-off policy has been. For instance, in *Simbi and the Satyr of the Dark Jungle*, which strikes a nice balance in the editing, we find these wonderful locutions unchanged, though they are none of them "correct": "perplexly" (for "perplexedly"? and "whisperly," a triumph for which there is no standard counterpart. "Hurthing here and there" (for "hurtling"?) seems to be justified somehow, though it is hard to say why.

This writer is somewhat troubled by the cryptic epigraphs under the chapter headings in *The Brave African Huntress*. If Tutuola ever is served by a Tutuola Society, such a group could exercise its ingenuity for quite a while, on some of these epigraphs, since some of them are very obscure. But perhaps the publishers could not throw their weight around and "persuade" the gentle Tutuola to drop these epigraphs or make them clearer, and some of them are interesting and impressive in their gnomic wisdom: "There is no another thought when hunger enters the stomach," "We must first greet the mother of a new born baby whether her baby will die soon or not," "Animals surplus in the town where the people have no teeth." Probably a case could be made for the conventional punctuation of Tutuola's sentence fragments, especially in *Feather Woman of the Jungle*. Of course it is perfectly easy to get used to stretching the sense over the periods, but it is a nuisance: "As the man had told me that he was the king and that house was his palace. So when I went round the house, it showed that it was a beautiful palace before. Because everything that I saw in it were belonged only to a king, but all were very old, and were nearly eaten off by the insects."

IX *Critical Responses*

The question of how and to what extent pidgin and broken English ought to be used in Afro-English fiction is associated with some very interesting theoretical considerations concerning language usage in fiction. Probably no reader would object to African characters using pidgin or broken English; after all, real Africans often speak thus, and it is generally agreed that the language of fictional characters should be appropriate to their educational and social circumstances. In this connection it is interesting to note that a theater group at the University of Ibadan has experimented with the use of pidgin in comedy.[32]

Also, most readers readily accept nonstandard English from the first-person narrator, reasoning, we may suppose, that this first-person narrator is also a character and so must use language suitable to his condition in life. Twain's *Huckleberry Finn*, we recall, has a narrator using a variety of American vulgate. But readers are uncomfortable or shocked if the author's voice in third-person narration or commentary is not in standard English, and they would probably be similarly upset if they thought that the author himself spoke the dialect or pidgin or broken English of his first-person narrator. Of course as long as the readers can have the comfortable feeling that the author does not think and speak, and usually write, in this kind of English, they will not object.

But the literary distinctions and judgments outlined above are not very consistent, really. If pidgin, broken English, or other nonstandard English is objectionable in the author's voice in third person, presumably because such English is not properly expressive —cannot say what needs to be said with subtlety, exactness, grace—

then the same objections would apply to that kind of English in the speech of the first-person narrator, for all that the novel says is said in this language. Or are we to assume that a writer normally speaking standard English can use nonstandard English better than the normal speakers of those forms? It seems a dubious assumption.

All but one of Tutuola's novels (*Simbi and the Satyr of the Dark Jungle*) are written in the first-person point of view, and most of his readers know that Tutuola does think, speak, and write in the "broken English" used by Drinkard and his other narrators. So readers who object to Tutuola's language must feel that speaking "junior clerk English" is somehow artistically crippling, that for the author who stands behind the narrator, as it were, to use the kind of English its narrator uses sabotages the artistic processes and distorts communication.

We used to believe that it was impossible for certain "primitive" languages to convey certain complicated modern concepts; linguists now tell us that the notion is pure superstition. Pidgin and an individual brand of "broken English" are consistent systems: we ought to be chary about predicting beforehand what they can convey and what they can't. The fact is that Tutuola's English is clear, forceful, and effective. It simply will not wash to suppose that critics like Dylan Thomas and V. S. Pritchett were bemused by the strangeness and quaintness of Tutuola's English.

We may wonder if social snobbery is not on this issue spoiling literary judgments. Since language variations are signs of status differences, and we assign a relatively high status to writers, our feelings of social propriety are offended when we hear the author's voice speak dialect, pidgin, or broken English, or when we understand that a fictional narrator's creator himself—oh horrors—speaks "awful English." Or perhaps intellectual snobbery is involved: woe be to the unlettered genius who presumes to engage in *belles lettres*. Surely we should allow off-beat English in first-person narration, even if it represents the language of the author; we should allow the author's voice to speak any kind of English but dull and dead English. As a matter of fact, might we not conceive of an author who speaks standard English *assuming* a nonconventional variety of English like Tutuola's for his author's voice in the third person? After all, the real living author and the author speaking in his novel are two quite different persons, and interesting effects might be secured by assuming a wilder brand of English, if it had the power and charm of Tutuola's!

The South African writer Ezekiel Mphahlele, writing in the *Harvard Educational Review* of Spring, 1954, can see no future for either pidgin or "broken" English in Anglo-African literature.[33] Mphahlele maintains that Nigerian pidgin has no "fixed grammar," but surely he must be wrong, for if pidgin communicates it must be structured, must be a regular system. Even Tutuola's English has a fixed grammar, though it varies consistently from standard grammatical forms. Mphahlele points out that pidgin is not spoken in Nigerian homes, as the Krio of Sierra Leone is. The argument seems to be that pidgin is a commercial lingua franca, a public patois. But drama and the novel are public forms too.[34]

Probably Mphahlele's most weighty objection to the use of pidgin in literary works is extra-literary, almost extra-linguistic. Africans want to "become literate," "to master the linguistic tools by which we can seize power in the broadest sense of the word. Standard English provides these tools most readily as the language of science, technology, the arts and so on." [35] We might say that although standard English does give an entrance into the Western arts and sciences and pidgin does not, pidgin might do better justice to many peculiarly African experiences than standard English does. Moreover, "mastering linguistic tools to seize power in the broadest sense of the word" sounds like a magical view of language: speak the European's language and presto! get his demonic technological power!

Not surprisingly, Mphahlele thinks Tutuola's species of English is just as unsuitable as pidgin for literary works: Tutuola's "unintentionally ungrammatical" manner (schoolmarm talk for nonstandard English) will somehow not be able to "catch on" and grow "into a conscious style in the hands of a more educated sophisticated writer." Mphahlele grants that Tutuola's manner is refreshing for readers weary of standard English, even readers of *Ulysses* and *Finnegans Wake*. It is the "primitive touch," though, that attracts the "non-Africans," and Africans would not want to use Tutuolese in literary works for the same reason that they would not use pidgin.[36] Incidentally, the Nigerian Gabriel Okara's mode of translating Ijaw idioms literally into English is "too strenuous," and it makes English a "slave" of the native language; the Ghanaian Efua Sutherland's device of suggesting the rhythm of her native language in English is "too sweet and pretty" for long narration.[37] According to Mphahlele, those writers most successful in adapting English for African needs are his compatriots, the black South Africans, using an English based on the speech of the people, an English which approximates the effects in native languages. Strangely, to write this kind of experimental style with "jazzed up" rhythm, African writers have to "forget grammatical or idiomatic English." [38] But how exactly is this English different from Tutuola's? Not quite so much "grammar" and "idiom" forgotten?

We can readily agree with Mphahlele that ideally African writers should exercise their "freedom and inclination to experiment" with the support of an African audience, rather than a European or American one. And certainly he is right in saying that these experiments will be coterie exercises, idle self-indulgence, unless the writers get the support of the people. Just possibly the people may use English as a political medium only, as they do in much of Africa now, or turn to the competing native languages, as might happen in South or East Africa.[39] Yes, African writers do need African readers, so that foreigners' tastes do not dictate the demand for books; and yet Mphahlele is not very convincing when he objects to all use of pidgin or nonstandard English in African literature.

Perhaps literary criticism needs something like a Theory of Creative Mistakes. One axiom of our theory might affirm that if a considerable number of speakers make the mistakes in question, they are not in fact mistakes but features of one of the many dialects or varieties of English. That is, much of Tutuola's English is not "bad English" but the vulgate English of Southern Nigeria. Other axioms in our theory might establish that "mistakes" or unconventional variations that make for conciseness in syntax, for additional nuances in the meaning of words, for wit and word play and delightful surprises—just those qualities that we noticed in Tutuola's English— are to be resolutely admired. Our theory might take notice of the fact that novelty of language arouses readers' interest and tends to make for slower, more deliberate, more alert reading. Of course our theory will have to admit that exotic English is not admirable when it is not clear and further that hitherto there has been a kind of literary convention that the professional writer, with the possible exception of American humorists, must, when he speaks in his own voice, use Queen's English.

Wole Soyinka, the young Nigerian poet and playwright, once wrote in a mimeographed student literary magazine that Tutuola's "wildly spontaneous kind of English hit the European critics at their weakest point—boredom with their own language and the usual quest for new titillations." Very well, but "wild spontaneity" *is* a virtue in a style, and languages *do* get boring, boredom being a natural disease of literary language. If educated Nigerians do, as Martin Banham judges, consider English something to "make and keep pure," then Americans and Europeans would do well to consider it something to make and keep fresh and free. Banham reports that Nigeria, far from being bored with English, is not even quite used to it. Well, then, perhaps restraint and discipline are proper for most Nigerians in the use of the language, but the "wild spontaneity" of Tutuola puts the English language in his debt.

Of course it must not be supposed that Nigerian writers cannot write standard English, that the new Nigerian literature in English is all written in an off-beat English. It is true that some earlier Nigerian writers, like those angry young nationalists A. A. Nwafor Orizu and Mbonu Ojike, besides writing a rather rococo English studded with quotations ranging from the Hebrew prophets to Harold Laski, pushed the English idiom pretty hard and were not always entirely intelligible.[40] But things are different now. The leading Nigerian novelist, Chinua Achebe, writes an admirable style— clear, warm, dignified, even grave—without being dull, and Achebe has to do so much with his English, must explain unobtrusively dozens of Ibo customs and beliefs and gather up and assimilate a quantity of Ibo terms and provincial sayings; in his second novel *No Longer at Ease* (1960), the sober standard English of the author's voice must march with the lively pidgin and vernacular English spoken by his characters.[41] Cyprian Ekwensi's novels have a few exotic touches like the police car "horning rudely," but whatever their faults of style, like occasional jargon ("roamed the Nigerian world"), literary inflation ("reeling bout of insatiable lust"), or poor taste ("felt his thick rough lips close on the nipple"), the author's voice speaks in genuinely idiomatic English.[42] The vernacular English and the pidgin spoken by the characters are particularly successful in Ekwensi's novels.

T. M. Aluko's novels have a rather undistinguished style, with more than their share of clichés and inappropriate diction, but their English is standard, and it often has a certain comic sparkle to it. The novels of Onuora Nzekwu are, in spite of the stilted dialogues and some rather wooden commentary in the second novel, *Blade Among the Boys* (1962), generally successful in their use of English; some of the conversation in his first novel, *Wand of Noble Wood* (1961), is quite spirited; much of the novel's commentary on Ibo customs and on the conflict between the traditional and the new religion is effective in an easy, helpful manner, though occasionally it lectures the reader. Nkem Nwankwo's English is faultlessly idiomatic in his novel *Danda* (1964); he is able to give the special flavor of Ibo speech by working Ibo words and expressions into his English: "You must take an *oibo* [European] name"; "But I will not tell you a lie, son of our fathers"; "Wait, men of our lands, I heard something today." [43]

But the reader may well wonder why a Nigerian literature must be written in any kind of English, pidgin or standard. Don't the Nigerians have their own languages? Indeed they do: they have about two hundred and fifty of them, some spoken by less than seven hundred persons. To be sure, the three most important languages—Yoruba, Ibo, and Hausa—have each of them perhaps ten million speakers, but the total population of Nigeria is estimated to be over fifty-five million. (Yoruba is spoken in the Western Region, Ilorin and Kaaba Provinces of the Northern Region, and the neighboring Republic of Dahomey; Ibo is spoken in the Eastern Region, the west bank of the Niger in the Western Region, and the southern part of Benue Province in the Northern Region; Hausa is spoken in the Northern Region and adjacent areas across the border in African nations of the French Community in the Western Sudan.)

We see the need for a common language in this situation. Making one of the indigenous languages official would stir up ethnic rivalries. English is the official language of the country's federal and regional legislatures, of its government agencies, of the major newspapers, of secondary schools, and of business and commerce. It is the language used by educated Nigerians, especially when speaking to members of other tribal groups or other African countries. It is of course the medium by which educated Nigerians make contact with the arts and sciences of the West. In the form of pidgin, English has wide currency among the common people, especially in the towns. Professor Banham has told this writer that the Nigerian novelists Ekwensi, Achebe, and Nzekwu, whom he knows personally, would not think of writing in their vernacular languages (they are all Ibos). [44]

Achebe's *No Longer at Ease* suggests the complexity of language use in Nigeria. The truck driver speaks pidgin to his passengers; the passengers sing in Ibo; the unheroic hero Obi, listening to the songs, translates them into English and interprets their subtle meaning, thinking in English. In his village home Obi reads an Ibo Bible at the family prayer service (and mispronounces his Ibo badly). He speaks standard English to his friends, to his girl friend, who is only part Ibo, and to his secretary in his office, but Ibo to a client who has broached a delicate matter (an offered bribe). The eloquent, proverb-laden speeches of the Umuofia Progressive Union, a sort of club for townsmen from an Ibo village sojourning in the big city, are in Ibo with occasional slips into English.

Perhaps this is the place to touch upon the relative merits of Anglo-African and vernacular African literature. It is true that writing in a second language, and writing for foreigners rather than one's own people, produces language distortions and may be somewhat inhibiting. It may well be, also, that a shortage of critics among the readers of the African vernaculars has tended to obscure the literary merit of much vernacular literature. For instance, this writer has often heard high praise from educated Yorubas for the Yoruba romances of Mr. Fagunwa. But most of the articulate critics of this world are innocent of Yoruba. And admittedly the size of the Yoruba readership has no bearing on the literary merit of the Yoruba vernacular literature.

But a case may be made for our encouraging (among other ways by sensible criticism) African literature in English. More than once in this study it has been urged that the Nigerian novelists, especially Tutuola, have enriched our language, now a world language which does not belong exclusively to the English and American descendants of the Angles and the Saxons. These novelists have exercised the humanizing effects of literature, not just in Yorubaland and Iboland but over the vast English-speaking area (and in western Europe through translations). By interpreting Nigeria to the West they have played a part in one of those hopeful ecumenical movements reconciling men of alien cultures. Besides being highly interesting examples of artistic acculturation, the Nigerian novels have perhaps served to radiate Nigerian cultural ideas upon our Western culture, with stimulating effect. Probably Africa needs two kinds of literature, each serving a different purpose: one an in-group literature for the exclusive use of Yorubas and Ibos and so on, the other an outward-looking literature addressing itself to the world and explaining Africa to the world.

Tutuola's Literary Powers

IT is now time to tally up and consider some of Tutuola's powers and graces, which will make or have already made him a classic in Afro-English literature. In doing so, we might well remind ourselves that several centuries of the dominance of the realistic tradition in the English novel have tended to deprive readers of the pleasure available in fantastic fiction like Tutuola's. In Tutuola's fiction the imaginatively conceived monsters, the fanciful transformations, and other marvels of oral literature are somehow intellectually refreshing, like brainstorming sessions, utopian thinking, and the wild absurdities of *risqué* jokes. It would seem that our minds are in danger of getting petty and stuffy if we feed too regularly on commonplace reality (perhaps the "fairy tales" of science also keep minds less stodgy).

I *The Marvelous*

Tutuola's work is of course jampacked with monsters and marvels to give us this sort of mental fillip. What reader, no matter how badly given over to the "mimetic fallacy," could fail to be stimulated by such matters as the self-beating drum that sounds like the efforts of fifty drummers, the free-loaders' hostelry-cum-mission-hospital in the huge white tree, the exhibition of smells, the woman-hill with noisy hydra heads and fire-flashing eyes, the stumpy, weepy-eyed, ulcerous Television-handed Lady, and the concert hall of birds with a guard company of white-shoed ostriches? [1]

And the transformations! There is somehow a pleasure in the very idea of a metamorphosis, as the continuing popularity of the Greek myths and of Ovid's classic on transformations attest. Like many of the transformations in the traditional tales (and some of those in the Grimms' collection), Tutuola's changes are good fun; for instance, Drinkard's changing himself into a canoe by which his plucky little

wife earns ferrying charges, his changing himself into a pebble and throwing himself ahead of the pursuing mountain creatures (an improvement over a traditional motif), Simbi's changing herself into a water insect so she can crawl up the Satyr's nostril and sting him to death, and Feather Woman's changing her victims into mud statues which (or who) can still feel and suffer.[2]

The appeal of these monsters and marvels is not escapist—that is, psychologically harmful. Tutuola's dream world is every bit as difficult for human intelligence and courage as our real world. The difficulties are often different in kind from those in the real world and so are many of the means of opposing the difficulties, but the human qualities are much the same. And, in a sense, modern science and technology—and their own ingenuity—will one day provide the Nigerians with marvels almost as incredible as those in Tutuola's novels.

II *Self-Assurance*

Even those critics and readers who do not care for Tutuola's work are likely to admit that he has one characteristic strength—his self-assurance, his literary aplomb, or composure. In spite of the junior clerk English with its distracting nonstandard syntax and vocabulary, in spite of the oddities of typography, in spite of the wildly mythical mode of fiction, Tutuola's authorial voice is magnificently composed, compellingly assured, like some oracle in the heyday of oracles, or like the passionate speech of a man speaking from lifetime convictions. We can note this quality, together with the accompanying oddities, in some of the opening passages of his romances:

I was a palm-wine drinkard since I was a boy of ten years of age. I had no other work more than to drink palm-wine in my life.

Simbi was the daughter of a wealthy woman, and she was an only issue of her mother.

She was not working at all, except to eat and after that to bathe and then to wear several kinds of the costliest garments.

I, Adebesi, the African huntress, will first relate the adventure of my late father, one of the ancient brave hunters, in brief:

My father was a brave hunter in his town. He had hunted in several dangerous jungles which the rest hunters had rejected to enter and even to approach because of fear of being killed by the wild animals and harmful creatures of the jungle.[3]

It is intriguing to try to account for this Tutuolan self-assurance.

Apparently Tutuola is one of those writers who "believe" their own stories. The *West Africa* correspondent who interviewed Tutuola reports that he "more than half-believes the tales he writes and he can, without mental trauma, reconcile this quasi-belief with his strong Christian views." [4] Perhaps the uncomplicated syntax without elaborate qualifications helps produce the effect—that, and the uncomplicated emotions felt by the main characters. But however we explain it, there it is, a monumental self-assurance, a steadfast, steady-as-she-goes self-assurance.

III *Memorability of Incidents*

Another of Tutuola's distinctive literary qualities, the memorability of his incidents, may be partly due to this verve and assurance, this sort of impetuous aplomb, and to his downright, no-nonsense style. Many of his incidents lodge fast in our consciousness; they stick like burrs in the memory. This writer drives by a limestone supply company and thinks of the nasty citizens of the "7th Town of Ghosts" who drink a urine and limestone mixture because water is "too clean for them." Driving across a long narrow bridge he thinks of the stick bridge over Lost or Gain Valley which is so fragile that travelers have to leave their clothes on the near side and take in exchange those they find left on the far side. In the midst of an acrimonious argument with a bigot, his mind is refreshed with the memory of the town of the "multi-coloured people" who hate the "mono-colour" of Simbi and her friends. A glance at the hideous expanse of paunchy male torsos at a beach calls up the grotesque scene in which the huge stern pigmy pushes the Brave Huntress along the road toward the pigmies' town—with his outsized navel. A row of statues in a museum brings back Feather Woman lashing her enchanted mud images until her fistful of switches are all broken. [5]

Although Tutuola is devoted to the mythical mode of thought, his works are full of graphic touches, clear and lively descriptions showing striking imaginative power, that should make the most inveterate partisans of realism lend momentary belief to his magical world. Telling detail of this sort is so commonplace that we have an embarrassment of riches from which to illustrate.

We can only offer a random sampling, reminding the reader that the illustrations will suffer considerable loss from being taken out of context. The king of the "field creatures," who menaces Drinkard and his wife, has a "hot steam . . . rushing out of his nose and mouth as a big boiler" and he is breathing "at five minute intervals." When

some person or creature in Faithful-Mother's huge white tree motions
with his hands that Drinkard and his wife should approach, each
of them wishes the other to go first: ". . . I myself pointed her to
the hands too; after that, my wife forced me to go first and I pushed
her to go first." [6]

During the first marriage of the wanderer in the Bush of Ghosts
Evil-of-evils shakes hands with him and gives him a shock like that
from a "live electric wire"; his friend has signaled him "with his eyes
not to shake hands with him to avoid the shock," but the wanderer-
bridegroom has not understood. When the same hero notices a very
short ghost at the foot of the tree in which he has been sleeping he
sees that she is "very corpulent as a pregnant woman who would
deliver either today or tomorrow." When Simbi and her adversary,
the satyr, are locked in deadly struggle, they hold each other very
tightly, and their eyes are open so wide with the strain that they
are almost ready ("nearly") "to tear like cloth." When the hollow
tree inside of which she has fallen catches fire from lightning, the
birds which have been nesting in the tree are frantic: "the eagles,
parrots, hawks, etc." are driven away by the smoke and the flame;
they "scatter" in the sky, then fly "round the top of the tree . . .
trying to take their young ones away from the smoke. . . ." [7]

In her fight with the pigmy guard with the "half fall goitre," the
Brave African Huntress and her enemy have "within a few minutes
. . . scattered away the dried leaves and refuses of that spot with
[their] feet." When the Chief Keeper of the "custody" brands the
Huntress on the forehead with three X's, the "rest of the two pigmies"
have to bend her head down first, because they are all so short. The
Feather Woman's teeth have fallen out, so that her mouth is "moving
up and down always as if she was eating something in the mouth."
The jaws of the starved villagers described in the fifth "entertainment" of *Feather Woman of the Jungle* have already "dried up like
roasted meat." The excited reaction to the earthquake produced by
the warriors of the Goddess of Diamonds in the seventh "entertainment" is reminiscent of the flurry caused by the fox in Chaucer's
"Nun's Priest's Tale"; it is a mad scene with the "dumps" (dumb)
murmuring, the "deafs" raising their "heads up to their Creator and
. . . expecting help from Him although they could not hear," the
cocks crowing, the elephants trumpeting, the "lames" creeping, the
dogs barking, the horses neighing, the cats jumping, the goats butting
the ewes, the rams scratching the ground "to escape into it," the bats
flying "all over the sky with fear." [8]

IV *Evocation of Terror*

Tutuola is a master in the evocation of the simple, uncomplicated emotion of fear. If in some romances terror is transmuted to delicious thrill, in Tutuola's romances it is terror pure—of course a vicarious literary version of it—much like the intense fear of nightmares. It is the fear of trapped, helpless humanity in the presence of, or in the grip of, bestiality and malignancy. Simbi inside the great hollow tree with the boa gliding toward her is typical; or the chief, treed by the "night woman" and her men, seeing his pursuers prepare to cut down the tree and tear him to pieces.[9] The fact that the incidents are hardly ever realistic does not keep them from giving the reader the vicarious terror: the vigor of the style, the graphic details, and the force and economy of the storytelling see to that.

Some critics have complained that Tutuola's horrors piled upon horrors become tedious, that his too closely packed episodes pall upon the reader. To a certain extent this is true, but these crowded, endless reels of frights and pursuits produce the nightmare atmosphere. For instance, a thinning out of the episodes in the short chapter "In the Spider's Web Bush" in *My Life in the Bush of Ghosts* would probably make the chapter a little less nightmarish. In the six and a half pages of the chapter, the wanderer is (1) chased by ghosts in an "alarm bush" (2) wound up in a spider web, as in a chrysalis (3) thus trapped, soaked by rain for three days (4) mistakenly buried as the body of the dead father of one of the spider-eating ghosts (5) dug up by a "resurrectionist" ghost and about to be eaten (6) burned in a fire while he effects his escape from three ghoulish ghosts about to eat him (7) while seeking shelter in a storm, carried off by a huge animal in whose pouch he has inadvertently taken refuge. Are not our own nightmares thus crowded?[10]

In Tutuola's episodes there is usually terror, and where there is no terror there is often anxiety. In his honeymoon with Super Lady, the wanderer in the Bush of Ghosts—feeling that the lady's bedroom is too grand for him and fearing her—is loath to lie down on her luxurious clean bed, so that she has to push him down on it "very gently as a breakable object." Tutuola's characters are hardly ever calm and at ease. In his nightmare world even the oddest-looking creatures are menacing, like the "half-bodied baby" with the "lower voice like a telephone," Faithful-Mother's White Tree, which "focuses" Drinkard and his wife, shouts at them in a voice that sounds as if it came from a tank, and flashes a stop sign, the "huge stern pigmy" with the herniated navel, the equestrian cudgel-bearer serving the Goddess of Diamonds, the Hairy Giant and Giantess of the underworld, the camel-riding archer. Funny-looking things and creatures in Tutuola's world are usually no joke.[11]

V Economy

A more sophisticated literary power of Tutuola's produces the dramatic impact of many of his incidents, especially in the last four romances. The actions and gestures in his later romances are as expressive as those in the first two romances, and in addition rather fewer episodes are more fully developed, with improved suspense, more conversation (delightful in itself but also sharply defining the conflict of characters), more exciting unexpected events, and more striking denouements. The other romances all contain about twenty episodes, but My Life in the Bush of Ghosts and all the later romances seem less crowded with episodes than The Palm-Wine Drinkard, without their losing the nightmare atmosphere. The romance with the fewest and best developed episodes is the next to the last: almost every one of the "entertainments" is restricted to one episode, and there are only ten "entertainments."

VI Surprise and Suspense

As we have observed, the conversational exchanges between Dogo the kidnapper and Simbi and between Satyr and Simbi are memorable; these battle dialogues are very spirited, and they serve admirably to characterize and to heighten the dramatic effect.[12] Delightful dramatic surprises would include Simbi's unwittingly killing her master by her singing, the Satyr's provision of an "illusive" concert hall complete with partially invisible orchestra and ostrich guards, the bugle speaking and "leaking out" the news of the King of Ibembe's horns while the African Huntress "winks her eyes" to warn the bugler, the chief keeper of the "custody" returning unexpectedly and finding the African Huntress drinking up his liquor, and the King of the Bush of Quietness confronting his wife and her lover's dead body (and her keeping the flies off the body).[13]

The suspense is well developed, among other instances, in Simbi's narrow escape from being sacrificed to the "spirit of the head" of the King of Sinners' town and from being executed as a thief by the King of the town of multi-coloured people, the terrified silence and the frenzied hiding of the people of Ibembe town, preyed on by the half-human bird, and the ominous hush of the Bush of Quietness entered by the chief-narrator.[14] Simbi's elaborate ruse for destroying her chief opponent, the Satyr, by flying up his nostril as a water insect, the African Huntress' escape from the "custody" by playing dead and being carried by the "pesters" out to the "place that they used to throw their deads," and the same heroine's escape from the ruined pigmy town by being hauled out by the "kind gorilla" would be fairly representative striking denouements.[15]

VII *Humor*

Tutuola's humor is one of his most ingratiating qualities, both the humor he draws from his traditional sources and that due to his own creativity. Although soliciting praise for one's own examples of a writer's humor is not a very promising business, humor is one of Tutuola's fortes and one likely to help him gain popularity, so we owe it to him to make the attempt. Sometimes it is the wild fancy that charms (a traditional Yoruba quality). In *The Palm-Wine Drinkard* the "complete gentleman," having won the affections of a lady "beautiful as an angel," returns his rented parts, limbs, "belly, ribs, chest, etc.," and is then reduced to a skull. (The episode is a very fine adaptation from traditional sources.) Drinkard, who modestly calls himself "father of gods who can do everything in the world," earns badly needed funds, as we have noted, by changing himself into a canoe ferrying passengers across a river; when his wife is swallowed by a "hungry-creature" he gets himself swallowed and fires his gun off in the creature's stomach. He escapes from the "mountain creatures," we remember, by changing himself into a pebble and throwing himself over the river (a bold improvement of his sources).[16]

As a sampling may indicate, the very fanciful variety and originality of the ghosts in the Bush of Ghosts are amusing: a copperish ghost, a silverish ghost, a golden ghost, handless, footless, and armless ghosts, naked ghosts, a smelling ghost, a "lower-rank" ghost, prominent ghosts, a homeless ghost, a famous ghost, "burglar" ghosts, a rich ghost, a "very beautiful young ghostess," a "jocose-ghostess," "triplet" ghosts, a very short ghost, ghost children, river ghosts (sometimes called aquatic ghosts or skeptical ghosts), the Super Lady Ghostess, the Rev. Devil Ghost, and the Television-handed Ghostess.[17] Odara in *The Brave African Huntress* keeps throwing his poisonous cudgels at the hunters though he is drowning. The pigmy gatekeeper quietly tells the huntress, "All right, come and lay your head on this rock and let me cut it off. I do not need yourself or rest part of your body but your head." The huntress, the junior keeper, and the stern pigmy all stand patiently at attention and in silence for two hours while the chief keeper finishes his drinking.

In *Feather Woman of the Jungle* the king of the savage people shouts so "terribly and loudly" that his voice shakes "the hills, rocks and trees. . . ." All the animals are so frightened that they become "mutes"; all the birds wake in their nests, and "all the rest living creatures" are so frightened that they are "unable to move their bodies" and they stand "still as if they [have] died." When this king, who walks with a walking stick made of human bones and rests his feet on a skull footstool, shouts a second time, his voice shakes the tree "so heavily" that the narrator falls out of the tree and on to the king. When a chief of this same savage people is tormenting the narrator by riding him horseback in a cave, the narrator tries to placate his tormentor by singing him a song, but the chief sings along with the narrator, singing a bass or a soprano (!) part; the chief enjoys himself so much that he jumps up and down in crazy joy, hitting his head on the roof of the cave. Tutuolan battle boasts come from the Hairy Giant in this romance: "Who are you? Who are you eating my mangoes: Stop in one place and let your death meets [*sic*] you or be running away and let your death chase you!" [18]

Much of Tutuola's humor is, of course, humor of hyperbole, which is also a traditional quality. A certain bush that Drinkard passes through is so thick that "a snake could not pass through it without hurt." A road he encounters is very lonely; no one passes on it, "even a fly did not fly on it." When the Red-king's subjects do not eagerly volunteer to be human (or should we say ghostly?) sacrifices to the local monsters, he offers the opportunity to Drinkard and his wife, and ". . . wanted to hear from [them] as soon as possible." In *My Life in the Bush of Ghosts*, when the hero screams during his baptism by fire and hot water, the ghosts answer unsympathetically, "You may die if you like, nobody knows you here." The hero's best man in his wedding to the beautiful ghostess is so bad that he has been "expelled from hell." In *Simbi and the Satyr of the Dark Jungle* the Satyr delivers himself of some pretty extravagant battle boasts, for instance, "Come along, my meat, I am ready to eat both of you now! Come along, and don't waste my time!" and "Certainly you have put yourselves into the mouth of 'death'! You have climbed the trees above the leaves!" *The Brave African Huntress* has an amusing summary of the quality of justice in the "custody": "Every mistake was a great offense and the penalty was to beat the offender to death at once." When required to choose a husband in Bachelors' town the huntress chooses a man she describes as "so old and weary that he could not even distinguish man from woman."[19]

But perhaps Tutuola's best humor is humor of situation. When Drinkard lets Death escape from the net in front of the house of the old man who has sent him to get Death, the old man and his wife make their getaway through the windows, and "the whole people in that town" run for dear life, leaving "their properties" behind. Drinkard has to judge a law case involving a "debiter" who has "never paid any of his debts since he was born," a bill collector who has "never failed to collect debts since he has begun the work," and a curious bystander who lingers on the scene to see the outcome of the encounter of the first two; the denouement of this little drama is alone worth the price of the book. For all the terror of the Bush of Ghosts humorous situations abound there. The golden, copperish, and silverish Ghosts have a ghostly brawl which only the superior dignity of Smelling-Ghost can put a halt to. Later the hero, transmogrified into the shape of a cow, shakes his head in agreement and disagreement with human arguments, talks cow talk which is "fearful" to his captors, and "also not clear to them." On another occasion his screams from a hollow log in which he is "corked tightly" seem delightful "lofty music" to the "homeless ghost" and his convivial friends. When Invisible Pawn puts a ghost head on the hero's shoulders, after the Ghost War, the hero is troubled by a compulsion to say things he does not mean to say, especially his "secret aims." In Hopeless-town he does poorly trying to talk in the shoulder-shrugging language that is locally current: he shrugs to the monarch of the place the tactless remark, "You are a bastard king." [20]

The humorous situations in *Simbi and the Satyr of the Dark Jungle* are less frequent, but choice. When Simbi's friend the snake-gnome removes the multi-coloured king's treasure, that autocrat's court is in a fine panic: a terrified bell-ringer lies prostrate, momentarily expecting the king to "behead him or send him to somewhere." Obsequious courtiers (and no courtiers are more obsequious than old-time African ones) scramble for the privilege of blowing the smoke out of the ceremonial pipe, and hold it while the king smokes, the bell-ringer being prostrate all the while. A later humorous situation concerns the tyranny of beauty. Two love-stricken young men carry Simbi and her friend Rali through the hostile Sinners' town; she has asked them "sharply with her attractive voice," and they have, in charming Tutuolan officialese, "lost all their senses in respect of the two ladies." When the Brave African Huntress Adebesi challenges her, the "bad semi-bird," in a burst of outraged self-esteem, shrieks (somewhat immodestly) that she is a wonderful bad creature who is half-human and half-bird and that she is so "bad that she is customarily eating together with witches." Before the stern pigmy can accost Adebesi she gets in the first word, "By the way, you this stern pigmy, what are you shouting for? You hopeless thing!" The king of the pigmies, who is old and half-blind, tries to shake hands with her captor, congratulating him, and shakes hands with Adebesi herself. But perhaps the funniest situation in the romance is Adebesi's drinking the chief-keeper's liquor while he is out on inspection and her being caught at it. Adebesi's sneaking the drinks, the keeper's incredulous astonishment at such boldness, and his throwing her "from the room to the outside of the office" and ordering his subordinates to beat her to death "at once"—it's all very fine humor of situation.[21]

The next romance has as many humorous situations as the others. Consider, for instance, the ludicrous aspect of the narrator's painful position when the Feather Woman has changed him into a mud image: his sister's suitor, a prince, ties his horse to the image and the horse kicks the narrator, bites him, "snorts" on his body, and scratches the image's head with his "snout." Before the narrator answers the Goddess of Diamond's questions about him, he gives himself the satisfaction of sitting down in one of her diamond chairs. When he seems covetous of her diamonds, she complains, "I wonder, why every human being never satisfy with whatever his Creator had provided for him," and the narrator replies, pertly but pertinently, "That was how our Creator had created all human beings." As the Hairy Giant and his hairy wife run out of their cottage in hot pursuit of the narrator, they collide in the narrow doorway—as in a movie cartoon comedy—and knock their heads together. The narrator and his wife Sela return to the domain of her mother, the Goddess of Diamonds; the old lady is so blind that she hires the couple as cleaners.[22]

VIII *Humanity*

But Tutuola's most important literary virtue is what we must call, for lack of a better term, his humanity—his compassionate view of human beings and his dramatizing and offering for his readers' admiration some of the saving traits of humanity: courage, resolution, persistence, ingenuity, resourcefulness, tolerance, kindness, and forbearance. His main characters, untrammeled by the usual human modes of moral bondage, are free from such idolatries as the devotion to slogans and fanatical ideals, to a domineering god or gods, to social standards, to war, to tribal traditions, to class mores, to sexual demands. They exhibit, after their own fashion, not a few of the cardinal virtues ascribed to the heroes and heroines of *Pilgrim's Progress* or *The Faerie Queene*—works in which, it might be added, monstrous elements exist in great abundance. It is impossible to illustrate by quotations these traits of Tutuola's heroes and heroines —Drinkard and his wife, the nameless wanderer in the Bush of Ghosts, Simbi and her friends, the African Huntress, and the story-telling chief—but by this time the reader will have noticed the traits in materials illustrating other matters.

It might be objected that these simple, uncomplicated virtues of Tutuola's characters are more admirable and pertinent in Tutuola's mythical world of physical and magical conflict with demons and ghosts than they are in our real world with its painfully complex moral conditions and its conflicts on so many different planes and in so many different relations. But surely simple virtues may have complicated applications, and just as surely in our day we are continually in danger of sophisticating our virtues into outright vices.

It might also be objected that a paralyzing fear in Tutuola's characters makes the moral atmosphere of Tutuola's mythical world unwholesome. It is true that fear is almost constantly in the minds of Tutuola's heroes and heroines and that this fear inspires in them some very rough combat tactics. On the other hand, this fear does not debase or brutalize the characters, or make them mean, suspicious, and cruel. Toward human beings, Tutuolan heroes and heroines are almost always generous, open, and kindly. Toward demons and hostile ghosts, they are at least open and aboveboard in their hostility.

One of the most striking peculiarities of Tutuola's protagonists is that they are wonderfully free from rancor and the desire for revenge. Drinkard does not harbor a grudge toward the old man who sends him to capture Death, and he does not brood over the incredible troubles brought on him by his monstrous "half-bodied baby." The wanderer in the Bush of Ghosts does not cherish his resentment of Smelling-Ghost, who mistreats him badly, or of the "homeless ghost" who "corks" him in a hollow log, or of Rev. Devil, who baptizes him with fire and hot water, or even of his wife, who displays a "rude attitude" to him and drives him out of town. Simbi shows no rancor for those who send her down a river nailed in a coffin, or for her mad friend who knocks out several of her teeth, or even for the Satyr himself, who has tortured her horribly.[23] The Brave African Huntress does not deeply resent the deadly pursuit of the outraged supporters of the King of Ibembe; she is very cool about the cruelty of the guards at the "custody" and she blames only herself for her sad fall from the good fortune of Bachelors' town. Similarly the story-telling chief does not think of revenge against the Feather Woman, a witch who has practiced several sorts of deviltry against him; he does not bother to entertain rancorous thoughts about the Goddess of Diamonds, who shakes up his property with an earthquake and has his wife abducted.[24] In spite of the superficial paganism of Tutuola's romances, there are clear reflections of his Christian beliefs and his personal gentleness.

What then is the significance of Tutuola's work? He has made available to the world the human values of the Yoruba folk tales, in the way the folk tale collectors could never do. He is in the true Yoruba tradition of the professional storytellers, the *akpalo kpatita,* but he performs in every place in the world where there are readers. This fairly catholic reader believes Tutuola's work will endure for the vigor and interest of his language (never mind the errors and hardly ever mend them!), the force and economy and dramatic effect of his storytelling, his fertile imagination, his graphic descriptions, his wild humor, the compelling power of his nightmare flights, tortures, horrors, ogres, and transformations, and the great humanity of his gentle Christian soul, unembarrassed by the African past, Western technology, or indeed anything else. Surely one day Amos Tutuola will be recognized as West Africa's first classic in world literature.

Notes and References

Titles of Tutuola's works are abbreviated as follows:

BAH—*The Brave African Huntress*
FWJ—*Feather Woman of the Jungle*
MLBG—*My Life in the Bush of Ghosts*
PWD—*The Palm-Wine Drinkard*
SSDJ—*Simbi and the Satyr of the Dark Jungle*

CHAPTER ONE

1. *FWJ*, p. 7.
2. "Portrait: A Life in the Bush of the Ghosts," *West Africa*, XXXVIII (May 1, 1954), 389. In his autobiographical note to the Grove Press edition of *The Palm-Wine Drinkard* (New York, 1953), Tutuola implies that Mr. Mornu supported his schooling from the start, when he entered the Salvation Army School. Mr. Dalley (note the different spelling) is not mentioned as a school patron and is called a father's cousin rather than an uncle. Tutuola's special promotion from Class I to Standard I "as I had the quicker brain than the other boys" probably took place in the Central School, though that school is not mentioned in the Grove Press account. (*The Palm-Wine Drinkard* [New York: Grove Press, 1953] p. 126.)
3. *Ibid.*; extracts from Tutuola's biographical notes to his publishers, dated March 30, 1957; "A Short Biography," revised biographical notes to his publishers, dated July 14, 1964, pp. 1–2.
4. Eric Larrabee, "Amos Tutuola: A Problem in Translation," *Chicago Review*, X (Spring, 1956), 40.
5. *West Africa*, XXXVIII (June 5, 1954), 513.
6. *Ibid.*, 322.
7. *Ibid.*, 414.
8. Anne Tibble (ed.), *African-English Literature* (New York, 1965), p. 96; *Times Literary Supplement*, May 25, 1962, p. 369; *The Spectator*, CCVIII (May 4, 1962), 592; *New Statesman*, LXIII (May 11, 1962), 683; *New York Times Book Review*, November 2, 1958, p. 41; Tibble, p. 96.
9. "A Short Biography," p. 3.
10. *West Africa*, XXXVIII (May 1, 1954), 389–390.
11. Larrabee, p. 40.
12. Letter to the writer from Amos Tutuola, dated May 11, 1958.
13. *West Africa*, XXXVIII (May 1, 1954), 389.
14. *FWJ*, p. 108; J. D. Fage, *An Introduction to the History of West Africa* (Cambridge, 1962), pp. 88–91; Cyril Daryll Forde, *The Yoruba-Speaking Peoples of South-Western Nigeria* (London, 1951), p. 4; James C. Coleman, *Nigeria: Background to Nationalism* (Berkeley and Los Angeles, 1958), pp. 25–27; K. M. Buchanan and J. C. Pugh, *Land and People of Nigeria* (London, 1955), pp. 149–150, 208–209.

CHAPTER TWO

1. *MLBG*, pp. 87, 90, 113, 145.
2. *SSDJ*, pp. 16–20, 73–79, 122, 31–33, 41–49, 81–82, 105.
3. *BAH*, pp. 38, 75–76.
4. *FWJ*, pp. 28, 49, 116, 124.
5. *MLBG*, pp. 97–110; *BAH*, 75–82; *FWJ*, 14–35.
6. *BAH*, pp. 71–110, 112–149.

7. *FWJ*, pp. 41–52, 73–83, 89–96.

8. *Aspects of the Novel* (New York, 1927), pp. 103–118.

9. *PWD*, p. 32; *MLBG*, p. 68.

10. *SSDJ*, p. 8.

11. *BAH*, pp. 114, 115, 117.

12. *Ibid.*, pp. 40, 91.

13. *Ibid.*, pp. 145–150.

14. *Ibid*, pp. 50, 139.

15. *Ibid.*, p. 27.

16. *Ibid.*, p. 46.

17. *FWJ*, pp. 34, 97.

18. *Ibid.*, pp. 63, 81.

19. This analysis of Tutuola's management of point of view, like most of my speculations on this subject, owes a great deal to Wayne Booth's account of point of view in Chapter VI, "Types of Narration," in his stimulating and seminal *Rhetoric of Fiction* (Chicago, 1961).

20. Foreword to *MLBG*, p. ii; Gerald Moore, *Seven African Writers* (London, 1962), pp. 40, 42–43.

21. *PWD*, pp. 11, 17, 31, 35, 41, 71, 95, 46–50, 65–72, 75–83, 64, 102–125.

22. *MLBG*, pp. 56, 63–64, 81, 84, 85, 89–95, 96–111, 112–125, 136, 137–139, 139–143, 144–150, 150–166, 167–174.

23. *SSDJ*, pp. 15, 52.

24. *Ibid.*, pp. 43, 52, 94–96, 120, 129, 133.

25. *Ibid.*, pp. 39, 75–80, 102–103, 107–108, 114–120, 122–125, 110–113.

26. *Ibid.*, pp. 64–71, 81–88, 105.

27. *Ibid.*, pp. 53–54, 94–96.

28. *Ibid.*, pp. 27–28, 39, 108.

29. *Ibid.*, pp. 32, 44, 54, 79–80, 78, 80, 123.

30. *Ibid.*, pp. 131–133.

31. *BAH*, pp. 9–13.

32. *Ibid.*, pp. 14–21.

33. *Ibid.*, pp. 24–31, 32–40, 41–46.

34. *Ibid.*, pp. 50–52, 61–64, 65–70.

35. *Ibid.*, pp. 75–99.

36. *Ibid.*, pp. 81–82, 93.

37. *Ibid.*, pp. 100–106, 109–111, 113–120, 121–128, 140–142

38. *Ibid.*, pp. 133–136, 142–150.

39. *Ibid.*, pp. 85–86, 101, 145–146, 149–150.

40. *Ibid.*, pp. 55, 65, 102, 107, 116, 117.

41. *Ibid.*, pp. 16, 56, 65–66, 71.

42. *Ibid.*, pp. 32, 44, 120; "Akanji," *The Brave African Huntress* by Amos Tutuola, *Black Orpheus*, No. 4 (October, 1958), 51.

43. *BAH*, pp. 107, 113, 42–43, 121, 117.

44. *FWJ*, p. 68.

45. *Ibid.*, pp. 52–53, 84, 97.

46. *Ibid.*, pp. 94, 114, 131–132, 90, 130, 55.

47. *Ibid.*, pp. 11, 22–23, 35–36, 52–53, 66–67, 83–84, 96–97, 103–104, 112, 122–123, 132. The formula is missing in the eighth night's entertainment, p. 111.

48. *Ibid.*, pp. 11, 36, 85, 97, 104.

49. For a useful definition of the novel see Northrop Frye, *Anatomy of Criticism* (Princeton, 1957), p. 304.

50. *Seven African Writers* (London, 1962), pp. 442–443.

51. *Anatomy of Criticism*, pp. 33, 187; *SSDJ*, pp. 15–21; *PWD*, p. 10.

52. *Anatomy of Criticism*, p. 187.

53. Phebean Itayemi and P. Gurrey, *Folk Tales and Fables* (London, 1953).

54. *PWD*, pp. 11–15, 17–29, 31–38, 58–63, 65–72, 76–81, 93–95, 109–110, 117, 120–125.

55. *MLBG*, pp. 17, 30–50, 59–60, 67–80, 89–92, 102, 105–106, 108–109, 135, 144–155, 163, 171–172.

56. *SSDJ*, pp. 22, 25, 28, 31–40, 47, 55–63, 83–91, 105, 116, 123–124, 131–136.

57. *BAH*, pp. 18, 20, 25–31, 34–46, 50–54, 61–64, 67–70, 75–99, 105–106, 113–118, 120–150.

58. *FWJ*, pp. 14–26, 39–52, 60–64, 68–78, 89–103, 105–111, 118–122, 124–132.

59. Moore, pp. 44–49. See also Campbell, *The Hero with a Thousand Faces* (New York, 1949), pp. 109–120, 37n, 40–41, 325n, 33n, 90–96.

60. Moore, pp. 49–50.

61. *Ibid.*, pp. 51–54.

62. Rev. ed., 6 vols. (Bloomington, Indiana, 1955–58).

63. *PWD*, pp. 31, 39, 110, 117; *MLBG*, p. 42; *SSDJ*, p. 124.

64. "African Literature, First Generation," *New Republic*, CXLVI (April 23, 1962), 34.

65. *PWD*, 56, 42, 44; playbill for the Ogunmola Traveling Theatre's production of *The Palm-Wine Drinkard* in the Arts Theatre of the University of Ibadan, in honor of the prime minister of Nigeria.

CHAPTER THREE

1. See John V. Murra, "The Unconscious of a Race," *Nation*, CLXXIX (September 25, 1954), 261–262.

2. *West Africa*, XXXVIII (May 1, 1954), 390.

3. *PWD*, pp. 17–30; Ogumefu, *Yoruba Legends* (London, n.d.), pp. 38–40; Dayrell, *Folk Stories from Southern Nigeria* (London, 1910), pp. 38–41; Jablow, *Yes and No: Intimate Folklore of Africa* (New York, 1961), pp. 184–188. In our examination of Tutuolan and other versions of folk tales, there is always the possibility that what we take for Tutuola's improvements may in fact represent superior versions not located in the collections; praise would then be due to Tutuola's wise choices rather than his invention.

4. *PWD*, 31–38; Itayemi and Gurrey, pp. 46–50. In W. H. Barker and Cecelia Sinclair's *West African Stories* (from Ghana), Quarcoo Bah Boni is a precocious child-pest; he tricks a goat, a wolf, a tiger, a lion, and an elephant that are living together (London, 1917), pp. 147–153.

5. *PWD*, pp. 120–125; Dayrell, pp. 20–28; Ogumefu, pp. 80–84.

6. Barker and Sinclair, pp. 90–94.

7. *PWD*, pp. 113–114; Jablow, pp. 118–120.

8. *MLBG*, pp. 17–21, 169–174;

Itayemi and Gurrey, pp. 21–23.

9. *MLBG*, pp. 112–135; Walker and Walker, pp. 11–16.

10. *MLBG*, pp. 130–143; Itayemi and Gurrey, pp. 31–33.

11. *SSDJ*, pp. 55–63; Walker and Walker, pp. 163–166; Ogumefu, pp. 21–26.

12. *SSDJ*, pp. 78, 123–124; Itayemi and Gurrey, pp. 40–44.

13. Walker and Walker, pp. 19–21; *BAH*, pp. 112–119.

14. Walker and Walker, pp. 17–18; *FWJ*, pp. 53–58; *BAH*, pp. 66–69.

15. Barker and Sinclair, pp. 39–40; *FWJ*, pp. 67–82.

16. Itayemi and Gurrey, pp. 8, 10, 13; *PWD*, pp. 117, 10–11, 31–38, 110; Paul Raduc and James Johnson (eds.), *African Folk Tales and Sculpture* (New York, 1952), pp. 32–40; Jablow, 49–51; Blaise Andrars, *The African Saga*, trans. Margery Bianco (New York, 1927), pp. 63–65, 355–361.

17. The *West Africa* interviewer reports that when Tutuola reads his stories "his expressive hands gesture impatiently, miming the words. . . ." *West Africa*, XXXVIII (May 1, 1954), 389. On one occasion, Tutuola represents an improvised song in the traditional style, the song about chocolates, ice cream, and victory over the savage pigmies (*BAH*, p. 149). However, not even Tutuola fully represents the range of Yoruba stories: he has few love stories, or dilemma stories, or riddles; he apparently does not care for risqué stories. For an excellent account of the African storyteller's art, see Jablow, pp. 30–33.

18. E. N. Obiechina, "Transition from Oral to Literary Tradition," *Présence Africaine*, English Edition, LX (1967), 143–4; Cyprian Ekwensi, *People of the City* (London, 1954), *Jagua Nana* (London, 1961), *Beautiful Feathers* (London, 1963), *Iska* (London, 1966); Chinua Achebe, *Things Fall Apart* (London, 1958), *No Longer*

at East (London, 1960), *Arrow of Gold* (London, 1964), *A Man of the People* (London, 1965); Onuora Nzekwu, *Wand of Noble Wood* (London, 1961), *Blade Among the Boys* (London, 1962), *High Life for the Lizards* (London, 1965).

19. Forster, pp. 159–160.

20. Franz Kafka, *The Penal Colony*, trans. Willa and Edmund Muir (New York, 1948), pp. 67–132.

21. *PWD*, pp. 8–9, 20, 120–122; *MLBG*, pp. 63, 73, 135; *SSDJ*, pp. 24, 33–34; *BAH*, p. 119; *FWJ*, pp. 44, 80.

22. Ulli Beier, "D. O. Fagunwa," No. 17 (June, 1965), 51–56; letter from Ulli Beier of Nov. 7, 1966. Wole Soyinka has translated a Fagunwa extract in *Black Orpheus*, No. 15 and Ulli Beier has a translation in the *Black Orpheus* anthology of McGraw-Hill (1965). Incidentally, Tutuola moralizes on at least one occasion, his story "Don't pay bad for bad" about two "tight friends," Dola and Babi, whose quarrels almost end in tragedy (*Présence Africaine*, English Edition II, No. 30, 78–81).

CHAPTER FOUR

1. Murra, pp. 261–262.

2. *SSDJ*, pp. 21–22, *BAH*, pp. 85–94.

3. *Aissa Saved*, Carfax ed. (London, 1952), p. 85.

4. *MLBG*, pp. 17–18.

5. Fage, pp. 88–91; Forde, p. 4.

6. *PWD*, pp. 65–73.

7. *FWJ*, p. 107.

8. *PWD*, pp. 26, 30, 27, 10, 28, 42; 28, 108; 23, 48, 51, 57, 84.

9. *Ibid.*, pp. 18–20, 31, 35, 42, 49–50, 52, 75, 102, 106, 120.

10. *MLBG*, pp. 36–37, 42; 112, 118, 124; 74, 75–76, 141; 25; 109; 66.

11. *Ibid.*, pp. 27, 34, 84–85, 86–87, 105, 125, 126, 129, 131, 154–155, 179.

12. *SSDJ*, pp. 23–124, 96, 122; 56, 61, 107–108.

13. *BAH*, pp. 110, 48, 113–119; 42,

46; private letter of May 11, 1958.

14. *FWJ*, pp. 57, 60, 72–76, 82, 107–108, 110–111, 112.

15. *PWD*, pp. 54, 66–67, 77–80.

16. *MLBG*, pp. 29–42, 39, 59–60, 67, 92, 161, 73–74; 97–100.

17. *SSDJ*, pp. 72, 80, 109–116, 47–48, 66.

18. *BAH*, pp. 27–31, 48–54, 38–40, 61–64, 65–70.

19. *FWJ*, pp. 14–16, 20. In his short story version of this episode Tutuola has The Feather Woman change the brothers of Ashabi into ducklings ("The Duckling Brothers and Their Disobedient Sister," *Présence Africaine*, English ed., VIII, No. 36, 73 78).

20. *Ibid.*, pp. 97–101.

21. *Ibid.*, pp. 116, 119–122.

22. Letter of Madeleine Wheeler for Walt Disney Productions, Burbank, Calif., May 7, 1958; Alan Pringle, Faber and Faber, letter of July 7, 1964.

23. *Anatomy of Criticism*, p. 193.

24. Carl Jung, *The Archetypes and the Collective Unconscious* (New York, 1959), pp. 81–84, 214–215, 20–21, 25–32, 215–217, 162–178.

25. *MLBG*, p. 97; *FWJ*, pp. 18, 84; *PWD*, p. 67.

26. *MLBG*, p. 29; *SSDJ*, p. 73.

27. *PWD*, p. 107; *BAH*, pp. 27, 61–75.

28. *SSDJ*, pp. 56–61; *FWJ*, p. 114.

29. *PWD*, pp. 31–37, 102.

30. Letter from Ulli Beier from Oshogbo, Nigeria, undated, probably some time in 1963.

31. *PWD*, pp. 65–72.

32. *Ibid.*, pp. 72, 114, 120.

33. *MLBG*, pp. 59–63, 114–122, 132.

34. *Ibid.*, pp. 144–153.

35. *Ibid.*, pp. 35, 40, 52 (156), 63, 91, 93, 85, 96, 102, 105, 110, 131, 163, 154–155.

36. *SSDJ*, pp. 22, 23, 38, 92, 93, 102, 109, 61–62, 73, 103–106, 74, 25, 90.

37. *BAH*, pp. 28, 48, 92, 117, 149, 9, 61, 66, 85.

38. *FWJ*, pp. 13, 23, 56, 61, 94, 97, 107, 131, 74–75, 72, 90–91, 16, 105, 53, 67.

39. *PWD*, pp. 22, 35, 40, 54, 70, 80, 104; two other non-technical similes are "like a policemen" (44) and "cleared as a football field" (60).

40. *MLBG*, pp. 23, 27, 50, 61, 74, 99, 100, 101. Two non-technical Western similes are "as when soldiers are receiving their rations from an officer" (103) and "as clean as a football field" (98).

41. *SSDJ*, p. 83; *BAH*, pp. 25, 55, 56, 70, 147.

42. *FWJ*, pp. 21, 65, 73, 109.

43. *PWD*, pp. 46, 54, 64, 68.

44. *MLBG*, pp. 24–25, 67, 97–100, 161–163.

45. *SSDJ*, p. 75; *BAH*, pp. 66, 70, 97, 143.

46. *BAH*, pp. 55, 21, 74, 23, 94.

CHAPTER FIVE

1. Murra, pp. 261–262.

2. *Reconstruction in Philosophy* (rev. ed.; Boston, 1948), p. 127.

3. In a letter of May 11, 1958, Tutuola asked the writer to send him these books: J. R. Eaton's *Beginning Electricity* and Alfred Morgan's *The Boy's First Book of Radio and Electronics.*

4. *West Africa*, XXXVIII (May 1, 1954), 389.

5. (London, 1960), p. 21.

6. Basil Davidson, *The Lost Cities of Africa* (Boston, 1959) is good on the distortions that racial prejudice brought to the study of African history. William Fagg and Eliot Elisofson's handsome volume *Sculpture of Africa* (New York, 1958) should bring home to the most skeptical what Africa has done for world art. Any of the many excellent anthropological monographs available, like Daryl Forde's on the Yorubas (1951), are instructive on the intricacy of native social and political forms. Margery Perham's early collection of African biographies, *Ten Africans* (London, 1936), helps us understand the Africans' hunger for Western education and Western ways of life.

7. Melville Herskovits, *The Human Factor in Changing Africa* (New York, 1962), pp. 464, 433, 93, 103, 111, 443.

8. Peter Ritner, *The Death of Africa* (New York, 1960), p. 6; George Kimble, *Tropical Africa* (New York, 1960), II, 33–51.

9. Fage, pp. 84–87.

10. Quoted in Gerald Moore and Ulli Beier (eds.), *Modern Poetry from Africa* (London, 1963), p. 19.

11. T. M. Aluko, *One Man, One Wife* (Lagos, 1959); Cyprian Ekwensi, *Jagua Nana* (London, 1961); Chinua Achebe, *Things Fall Apart* (London, 1958); Moore and Beier, pp. 43–53. For a discussion of the attitudes of Nigerian novelists toward the African past, see my "The Novel in Nigeria" in *Writers the Other Side of the Horizon* (Champaign, Ill.: National Council of Teachers of English, 1964), pp. 51–58. The attitude of the distinguished young Nigerian dramatist Wole Soyinka toward the African past is very interesting: he is disenchanted with the African past and not overly hopeful about the African future. His well-known allegorical play *A Dance in the Forest* (1963) includes a flashback to the African past in which an honest captain refuses to lead his troops in a war to recover the personal effects of the despotic king's queen from her former husband, or to commit adultery with that queen as she suggests. The captain pays for his integrity by being sold into slavery and suffering emasculation. The courtiers are all obsequious and corrupt. However, Soyinka also sees plenty of corruption in modern Westernized Nigeria. A dishonest official has allowed a dangerous passenger lorry to operate on the roads, and it

burns, killing sixty-five passengers. A character called Forest Head, rather like the Christian God, complains of "The fooleries of beings whom I have fashioned closer to me weary and distress me. Yet I must persist, knowing that nothing is really altered" (Wole Soyinka, *A Dance in the Forest* [London, 1963], pp. 53–65, 15–18, 82).

CHAPTER SIX

1. *PWD*, p. 15.
2. *Black Orpheus*, No. 2 (1960, 1961?), p. 7.
3. Foreword to *MLBG*, p. x.
4. *West Africa*, XXXVIII (May 1, 1954), 389–390.
5. Moore, *Seven African Writers*, p. 77; V. S. Pritchett, *New Statesman and Nation*, XLVII (March 25, 1954), 291.
6. Moore, p. 42; Murra, 261–262; Pritchett, 291.
7. *PWD*, pp. 9, 18; *MLBG*, pp. 46, 80, 156; *SSDJ*, pp. 111, 118; *BAH*, pp. 44, 135.
8. *MLBG*, pp. 97–98; *SSDJ*, p. 75; *BAH*, p. 77; *FWJ*, p. 82.
9. *PWD*, p. 25; *MLBG*, pp. 25, 33; *SSDJ*, pp. 27, 78, 111, 120; *BAH*, pp. 43, 122; *FWJ*, pp. 27, 70, 123; *MLBG*, p. 24; *SSDJ*, pp. 41, 70, 118; *BAH*, pp. 131, 139; *PWD*, p. 10; *BAH*, p. 144; *SSDJ*, p. 7; *BAH*, pp. 34, 123; *SSDJ*, p. 17.
10. *MLBG*, p. 21; *SSDJ*, p. 72; *BAH*, p. 134; *PWD*, p. 9; *MLBG*, p. 133; *SSDJ*, p. 33, 96, 131; *FWJ*, pp. 25, 27, 87. Sometimes Tutuolan English has the regular verb form where standard English has the progressive: *as if many persons talked into a big tank* (*PWD*, p. 66). Occasionally Tutuola switches transitive forms to intransitive and intransitive to transitive: *rose up our heads, trespassed their town, I laid down, we had lost in jungle* (*PWD*, pp. 44, 45; *MLBG*, p. 95; *FWJ*, p. 21). Tutuola invents some new past participles and past tenses calculated to distress English teachers: *had al-*

ready dead, hill . . . *which splited or parted into two, span all to a single strong rope, ripen plantains, bursted in laughter* (*SSDJ*, p. 18; *BAH*, pp. 60, 104; *FWJ*, pp. 88, 112).
11. *PWD*, p. 7; *MLBG*, pp. 20, 24; *BAH*, p. 37; *FWJ*, p. 85.
12. *PWD*, p. 45, 93; *FWJ*, p. 56.
13. *PWD*, p. 15; *MLBG*, p. 154; *SSDJ*, p. 102; *BAH*, pp. 28, 118, 131; *FWJ*, p. 125.
14. *MLBG*, p. 32.
15. *FWJ*, p. 94.
16. *PWD*, pp. 63, 111; *FWJ*, p. 101; *MLBG*, p. 52; *SSDJ*, p. 79; *BAH*, p. 135.
17. *PWD*, pp. 18, 96; *SSDJ*, p. 104; *PWD*, p. 37; *MLBG*, pp. 18, 122, 156; *SSDJ*, p. 19; *BAH*, p. 37; *FWJ*, p. 76.
18. *PWD*, p. 69; *MLBG*, p. 48; *SSDJ*, pp. 7, 52; *BAH*, pp. 43, 62, 63, 118, 130, 136, 145; *FWJ*, pp. 15, 58, 112; *PWD*, pp. 34, 93; *MLBG*, p. 140; *SSDJ*, p. 39, Cf. These examples from a short story "Ajayi and the Witchdoctor": *explained quietly with tears, advised him softly, walked wildly* (*Black Orpheus*, No. 19 [March, 1966], 10–14).
19. *PWD*, pp. 19, 57; *SSDJ*, p. 47; see also *SSDJ*, pp. 104, 109.
20. *MLBG*, pp. 33, 67, 155; *BAH*, pp. 21, 74, 94, 102; *PWD*, p. 86; *MLBG*, pp. 146, 174.
21. *BAH*, pp. 24, 65; *PWD*, pp. 7, 86, 85; *PWD*, pp. 18, 110; *MLBG*, p. 21.
22. *PWD*, pp. 93, 95, 104, 120; *MLBG*, pp. 65, 146; *PWD*, p. 96; *MLBG*, p. 147.
23. *PWD*, pp. 46, 57, 67, 73, 83; *MLBG*, pp. 72, 114, 126, 112. Some other hyphenations: "DEAD-BABIES," "mountain-creatures," "unknown-mountain," and "jocose-ghostess" (*PWD*, p. 102, 115; *MLBG*, p. 121).
24. *FWJ*, p. 24.
25. *Ibid.*, p. 104.
26. *BAH*, pp. 65, 38, 40, 44.
27. Alan Pringle of Faber and Faber

has told the writer that "any clarification of the text in this office in the manner indicated on p. 24 of *The Palm-Wine Drinkard* has been kept to a minimum and I should say that less of it has been done or will be done in *Simbi and the Satyr of the Dark Jungle* and *The Brave African Huntress* than in the first two books" (Letter of Alan Pringle, April 30, 1957).

28. Other editorial emendations cannot be judged with much assurance because the original is not clear or we cannot be sure who made the corrections. The corrected form of "all the kinds of people in the market" was originally something undecipherable, perhaps "all the kind of the people." The editor's reading "and I cried for a few minutes, because I thought within myself why was I not created with beauty as this gentleman . . ." has been produced by changing an undecipherable compound conjunction (that ***) and transposing "I was not created." Is the "thought within myself" tautological? Or an excellent reminder of the inwardness of thought?

29. *PWD*, p. 38; *MLBG*, p. 61. Double quotation marks in the text. In the letter referred to above, Alan Pringle implies that Geoffrey Parrinder of the University of Ibadan edited, or helped to edit, *My Life in the Bush of Ghosts*: "With the exception of *My Life in the Bush of Ghosts*, Tutuola's books have not been edited by Geoffrey Parrinder."

30. *Black Orpheus*, No. 4 (October, 1958), 52–3.

31. *FWJ*, pp. 8, 111, 100, 128, 29; *Présence Africaine*, English edition, VIII (n.d.), 73. Other dubious uncorrected misspellings are *hot* for *hut* (*BAH*, p. 82) and *crambed* for *cramped* (*FWJ*, p. 85). We often run across intriguing problems in a Tutuola text. For instance, should "bugle the strong room" be "burgle the strong-room" as the sense seems to require? Have the words *bugle* and *bugle-blowers* confused the writer—or the editor? (*FWJ*, p. 79).

32. *SSDJ*, pp. 41, 104, 39; *BAH*, pp. 71, 65; *FWJ*, p. 48. A Nigerian student, commenting in a student literary magazine on Miss Yetunde Esan's pidgin comedy *Don't Say It in Writing*, observes that pidgin will be "a proper medium for comedy in Nigeria. . . . English is too remote for a drama that can belong to the people" (Martin Banham, "The Beginnings of Nigerian Literature in English," *A Review of English Literature*, III [April, 1962], 97). Obotunde Ijimere's interesting one-act play *The Fall* (Oshogbo, Nigeria, n.d.) uses pidgin effectively and so does his hilariously funny one-acter *The Suitcase* (Oshogbo, 1966).

33. XXXIV, 289–305.

34. *Ibid.*, 299.

35. *Ibid.*

36. *Ibid.*, 299–300.

37. *Ibid.*, 300, 304, 301.

38. *Ibid.*, 304.

39. *Ibid.*, 304–305.

40. A. A. Nwafor Orizu, *Without Bitterness: Western Nations in Post-War Africa* (New York, 1944); Mbonu Ojike, *My Africa* (New York, 1946).

41. *No Longer at Ease* (London, 1960).

42. *People of the City*, p. 24; *Jagua Nana*, pp. 173, 38, 126.

43. *Danda* (London, 1964), pp. 74, 117, 128.

44. James C. Coleman, *Nigeria: Background of Nationalism* (Berkeley, 1958), pp. 15–17. Frederick A. O. Schwarz, Jr., *Nigeria: The Tribes, the Nation, or the Race—The Politics of Independence* (Cambridge, Mass., 1965), pp. 2, 38–45, 141–142.

CHAPTER SEVEN

1. *PWD*, pp. 58, 68–73; *MLBG*, pp. 35, 96–104, 161–163; *SSDJ*, pp. 109–114.

2. *PWD*, pp. 39, 117; *SSDJ*, p. 124; *FWJ*, p. 19.

3. *PWD*, p. 7; *SSDJ*, p. 7; *BAH*, p. 9.

4. *West Africa*, XXXVIII (May 1, 1954), 389.

5. *MLBG*, pp. 39, 131; *SSDJ*, p. 52; *BAH*, p. 77; *FWJ*, p. 20.

6. *PWD*, pp. 46, 66.

7. *MLBG*, pp. 61, 63; *SSDJ*, pp. 79, 88.

8. *BAH*, pp. 63, 84; *FWJ*, pp. 15, 68, 99.

9. *SSDJ*, pp. 83, 86; *FWJ*, p. 57.

10. *MLBG*, pp. 89–95.

11. *Ibid.*, p. 120; *PWD*, pp. 35, 66; *BAH*, p. 77; *FWJ*, pp. 99–100, 114–122.

12. *SSDJ*, pp. 16–20, 73, 75, 122.

13. *Ibid.*, pp. 27, 109–114; *BAH*, pp. 44, 93; *FWJ*, p. 45.

14. *SSDJ*, pp. 39, 54–63; *BAH*, pp. 34–37; *FWJ*, p. 38.

15. *SSDJ*, p. 124; *BAH*, pp. 93, 105–106.

16. *PWD*, pp. 17–21, 39, 109–110, 117.

17. *MLBG*, pp. 24–25, 27, 29, 32, 39, 49, 52, 55, 56, 57, 59, 63, 65, 72, 83, 112, 129, 161.

18. *BAH*, pp. 31, 50, 82; *FWJ*, pp. 60, 63, 99, 116.

19. *PWD*, pp. 41, 56, 71; *MLBG*, pp. 60, 59; *SSDJ*, pp. 73, 75; *BAH*, pp. 89, 114.

20. *PWD*, pp. 15, 111–112; *MLBG*, pp. 28, 44, 47, 50, 109, 126–127.

21. *SSDJ*, pp. 58–59, 131; *BAH*, pp. 38, 75, 81, 93.

22. *FWJ*, pp. 31, 82, 90, 121, 131. The story "Ajayi and the Witchdoctor" has a grotesquely humorous situation: Ajayi is prepared to behead his own dead father as he comes out of his grave (*Black Orpheus*, No. 19 [March, 1966], 10–14).

23. *PWD*, pp. 16, 35–58; *MLBG*, pp. 29, 42, 49, 59–63, 135; *SSDJ*, pp. 29, 49–50, 122.

24. *BAH*, pp. 46, 85–94, 119; *FWJ*, pp. 33–34, 97–103.

Selected Bibliography

PRIMARY SOURCES

Ajaiyi and His Inherited Poverty. London: Faber and Faber, 1967.

"Ajantala and the Noxious Guest," in *African Treasury*, ed. LANGSTON HUGHES. New York: Crown Publishers, 1960; Pyramid Books, 1961. A lively story of a miraculous, mischievous child who mistreats Mr. Goat, Mr. Ram, and Mr. Lion; the child shares a name and several motifs with the Ajantala of an episode in *The Brave African Huntress*.

"Ajayi and the Witch Doctor," *Black Orpheus*, No. 19 (March, 1966), 10–14. Another, inferior version of this story appears in *Atlantic Monthly*, CCIII (April, 1959), 78–80. This earlier version of a tale about a poverty-stricken farmer's outwitting an unscrupulous witch doctor is less detailed, less well developed, but perhaps more characteristically Tutuolan in language. The *Black Orpheus* version appears virtually unchanged as the climactic episode in the last chapter of *Ajaiyi and His Inherited Poverty*.

"Amos Tutuola Tells a Story: 'Don't Pay Bad for Bad,'" *Présence Africaine*, English Edition, II, No. 30, 78–81. A story of trouble between two "tight" friends. With some slight stylistic changes and one changed name this story forms most of the seventh chapter of *Ajaiyi and His Inherited Poverty*.

"Amos Tutuola Tells a Story: 'The Duckling Brothers and Their Disobedient Sister,'" *Présence Africaine*, English Edition, VIII, No. 36, 73–78. A version of the first episode in *FWJ*.

The Brave African Huntress. London: Faber and Faber, 1958; New York: Grove Press, 1958.

"The Elephant Woman," *Chicago Review*, X (Spring, 1956), 36–39. This story appears in rather different form in *My Life in the Bush of Ghosts*, pp. 112–135.

Feather Woman of the Jungle. London: Faber and Faber, 1962.

"My First Wedding Day in the Bush of Ghosts," in *Darkness and Light*, ed. PEGGY RUTHERFOORD. London: Faith Press, 1958. (Published in United States as *African Voices*. New York: Vanguard, n.d.). An episode from *My Life in the Bush of Ghosts*.

My Life in the Bush of Ghosts. London: Faber and Faber, 1954; New York: Grove Press, 1954.

The Palm-Wine Drinkard. London: Faber and Faber, 1952; New York: Grove Press, 1954.

Simbi and the Satyr of the Dark Jungle. London: Faber and Faber, 1955; New York: Grove Press, 1962.

SECONDARY SOURCES

1. *Works by Other African or Expatriate Writers*

ACHEBE, CHINUA. *Arrow of Gold.* London: Heinemann, 1964. One of the very best of the Nigerian novels, a study of a cult priest's conflict with white authorities and his own tribe.

————. *No Longer at Ease*. London: Heinemann, 1960. Novel about the downfall of an educated Nigerian destroyed by bribe-taking; excellent picture of a tribal union.

————. *Things Fall Apart*. London: Heinemann, 1958. Achebe's best novel. Treats the collapse of Ibo culture and the downfall of an Ibo man of character with the arrival of the whites.

————. *A Man of the People*. London: Heinemann, 1966. Study of an engaging, corrupt Nigerian politician.

ALUKO, T. M. *One Man, One Wife*. Lagos: Nigerian Printing Co., 1959. Lighthearted comic novel spoofing both Western and traditional ways.

Black Orpheus. No. 9 (November, 1959), 33.

EKWENSI, CYPRIAN. *Beautiful Feathers*. London: Hutchinson, 1963. A rather slight novel about a Nigerian political leader.

————. *Iska*. London: Hutchinson, 1966. The amours of a Lagos model, the devotion of the Prayer People, and the deals of corrupt politicians.

————. *Jagua Nana*. London: Hutchinson, 1961. Lively novel about a Nigerian courtesan, conveys the rather squalid charms of Lagos.

————. *People of the City*. London: Dakers, 1954. Rather slight novel about a Lagos man-about-town; the Lagos setting is well done.

IJIMERE, OBOTUNDE. *The Fall*. Oshogbo, Nigeria: Adayemo Printing Press, n.d.

————. *The Suitcase*. Oshogbo, Nigeria: Adeyeye Printing Press, 1966.

MOORE, GERALD and ULLI BEIER (eds.). *Modern Poetry from Africa*. London: Oxford, 1963. Standard anthology of African poetry in the European languages.

NWANKWO, NKEM. *Danda*. London: Andre Deutsch, 1964. Successful Nigerian novel about young ne'er-do-well who fails by both traditional and modern standards of success.

NZEKWU, ONUORA. *Blade Among the Boys*. London: Hutchinson, 1962. A Nigerian novel overloaded with anthropological lore and poor in motivation.

————. *Wand of Noble Wood*. London: Hutchinson, 1961. Fairly successful Nigerian novel.

————. *Highlife for Lizards*. London: Hutchinson, 1965. Interesting novel about the married life of an Ibo woman.

OJIKE, MBONU. *My Africa*. New York: John Day, 1946. Early nationalistic polemical book.

OKARA, GABRIEL. "The Crooks," *Black Orpheus*, No. 2 (n.d., 1960? 1961?), 7. Nigerian story employing pidgin.

SOYINKA, WOLE. *A Dance in the Forest*. London: Oxford, 1963. Interesting symbolical Nigerian Play.

2. *Studies*

AKINJOGBIN, ADEAGBO. *West Africa*, XXXVIII (June 5, 1954), 513. Hostile review of *PWD* by a Nigerian who had not even read the romance.

BANHAM, MARTIN. "Beginnings of a Nigerian Literature in English," *Review of English Literature*, III (April 1962), 88–99. Review of Nigerian writers, including Tutuola.

BARKER, W. H. and CECILIA SINCLAIR. *West African Stories*. London: George G. Harrap, 1917.

BOOTH, WAYNE. *The Rhetoric of Fiction*. Chicago: University of Chicago Press, 1961.

BUCHANAN, K. M. and J. C. PUGH. *Land and People of Nigeria*. London: University of London Press, 1955. Standard work on the Nigerian background.

CAMPBELL, JOSEPH. *The Hero with a Thousand Faces*. (Bollingen Series VIII.) New York: Pantheon Books, 1949. Standard work on the subject but not easy reading.

CENDRARS, BLAISE (ed.). *The African*

Saga, trans. MARGERY BIANCO. New York: Payson and Clark, 1927.

COLEMAN, JAMES C. *Nigeria: Background to Nationalism.* Berkeley and Los Angeles: University of California Press, 1958. Standard work on modern pre-independence political background.

COLLINS, HAROLD. "The Novel in Nigeria," in *Writers the Other Side of the Horizon.* Champaign, Illinois: NCTE, 1964. Critical survey of Nigerian novels.

DAVIDSON, BASIL. *The Lost Cities of Africa.* Boston: Little, Brown, 1959. Describes the archeological record of civilization on the east coast of Africa.

DAYRELL, ELPHINSTONE. *Folk Stories from Southern Nigeria.* London: Longmans, Green, 1910.

ELISOFSON, ELIOT. *The Sculpture of Africa.* New York: Praeger, 1958. Splendid illustrations of African art in bronze and wood.

FAGE, J. D. *An Introduction to the History of West Africa.* Cambridge: University Press, 1962. Excellent introduction to the subject.

FORDE, CYRIL DARYLL. *The Yoruba-Speaking Peoples of South-Western Nigeria.* London: International African Institute, 1951. Standard anthropological study of Tutuola's tribe.

FORSTER, E. M. *Aspects of the Novel.* London: Harcourt, Brace and Co., 1927.

FRYE, NORTHROP. *Anatomy of Criticism.* Princeton: Princeton University Press, 1962.

HERSKOVITS, MELVILLE. *The Human Factor in Changing Africa.* New York: Knopf, 1962. Good on African contributions to world culture.

ITAYEMI, PHEBEAN and P. GURREY. *Folk Tales and Fables.* London: Penguin, 1953. Probably the collection Tutuola was accused of plagiarizing from; includes Yoruba section.

JABLOW, ALTA. *Yes and No: The Intimate Folklore of Africa.* New York: Horizon Press, 1961. Contains African proverbs and riddles.

JUNG, CARL, *The Archetypes and the Collective Unconscious,* (*Collected Works,* IX, Part I). New York: Pantheon, 1959.

KIMBLE, GEORGE. *Tropical Africa.* 2 vols. New York: The Twentieth Century Fund, 1960. Standard work on the geography of this area.

LARRABEE, ERIC. "Amos Tutuola: A Problem in Translation," *Chicago Review,* X (Spring, 1956), 40.

MACAULEY, ROBIE. "African Literature, First Generation," *New Republic,* CXLVI (April 23, 1962), 34. Survey of work of new African writers, including Tutuola, by editor of *Kenyon Review.*

MOORE, GERALD. "Amos Tutuola: Nigerian Visionary," *Black Orpheus.* No. 1 (n.d.). Splendid critical study, an earlier version of his chapter on Tutuola in *Seven African Writers.*

————. *Seven African Writers.* London: Oxford University Press, 1962. Includes a chapter on Tutuola, the best study of his works to date.

MPHAHLELE, EZEKIEL. *The African Image.* London: Faber and Faber, 1962. The image of the African in expatriate and African literature treated by refugee South African, sound and interesting.

————. "The Language of African Literature," *Harvard Educational Review,* XXXIV (Spring, 1964), 289–305.

MURRA, JOHN V. "The Unconscious of a Race," *Nation,* CLXXIX (September 25, 1954), 261–262. Sympathetic review of Tutuola's first two romances by an anthropologist.

OGUMEFU, M. I. *Yoruba Legends.* London: Sheldon Press, n.d.

PERHAM, MARGERY. *Ten Africans.* London: Faber and Faber, 1936. Splendid collection of autobiographies of emergent Africans.

"Portrait: A Life in the Bush of Ghosts," *West Africa*, XXXVIII (May 1, 1954), 389. An interview with Tutuola.

PRITCHETT, V. S. *New Statesman and Nation*, XLVII (March 25, 1954), 291. Sympathetic review of Tutuola's first two romances.

RADUC, PAUL and JAMES JOHNSON (eds.). *African Folk Tales and Sculpture*. New York: Pantheon, 1952. Handsome book with excellent collection of tales.

RITNER, PETER. *The Death of Africa*. New York: Macmillan, 1960. Pessimistic account of Africa's resources and prospects.

THOMPSON, STITH. *Motif-Index of Folk Literature*. 6 vols., rev. ed. Bloomington: University of Indiana Press, 1955–58. Monumental work documenting the universality of folklore motifs.

TIBBLE, ANNE (ed.). *African-English Literature*. New York: October House, 1965. Anthology with critical chapters.

TUTUOLA, AMOS. "Extracts from Author's Biographical Notes to His Publishers," March 30, 1957.

———. "A Short Biography," revised biographical notes to his publishers, July 14, 1964.

WALKER, BARBARA and WARREN. *Nigerian Tales*. New Brunswick: Rutgers University Press, 1961.

"Writing in West Africa: A Chance to Adapt and Experiment," *The Times Literary Supplement*, August 10, 1962.

Index

Achebe, Chinua, idiomatic English of his novels, 114; see also Attitude toward the African past

Africa, its equality or superiority in some areas of human endeavor, like politics, religion, the arts, and social organization, 90–91; its real backwardness in the sciences and technology, 91; its supposed general backwardness, 89–90; its technical backwardness, probably caused by the extremely harsh environment and by slavery, 92–93; the westerners' monumental ignorance and prejudice regarding African conditions, 90–91

Ajaiyi and His Inherited Poverty, plot summary of, ix–x; see also Characterization, Plot management, Point of view, and Romance quest

Aluko, T. M., idiomatic English of his novels, 114; see also Attitude toward the African past

Anxiety, evocation of, in the romances, 121

Attitude toward the African past, of Tutuola, 93; of Aluko, Ekwensi, Achebe, and Senghor, 94

Bachelor's town episode in *The Brave African Huntress*, compared with analogue in Walker collection of Nigerian folk tales, 59

Bad semi-bird, monstrous bird-human in *Simbi and the Satyr of the Dark Jungle*, 75

Bako, a demented young woman transformed to a rooster in *Simbi and the Satyr of the Dark Jungle*, described, 74

Beier, Ulli, on Tutuola's language, 100

Brave African Huntress, The, plot summary of, 28; see also Characterization, Plot management, Point of view, and Romance quest

Chairwoman of the witches, an ogress in *Ajaiyi and His Inherited Poverty*, ix

Characterization, in *The Brave African Huntress*, 29; in *Feather Woman of the Jungle*, 29–30; in *My Life in the Bush of Ghosts*, 28; in *The Palm-Wine Drinkard*, 28; in *Simbi and the Satyr of the Dark Jungle*, 28–29

Chief's dogs' saving him from the savage people, an episode compared with an analogue in the Walker collection of Nigerian folk tales, 60

Conventions in fiction regarding first-person narrators' and "omniscient authors'" use of nonstandard English, 111

Conversation, management of, in *Ajaiyi and His Inherited Poverty*, x; in *The Brave African Huntress*, 27; in *Feather Woman of the Jungle*, 27; in *My Life in the Bush of Ghosts* and *The Palm-Wine Drinkard*, 26; in *Simbi and the Satyr of the Dark Jungle*, 26–27

Creative Mistakes, Theory of, to help readers appreciate an unconventional writer like Tutuola, 113

Cultural independence of Nigerians, growing after political independence, 89

Daley (or Dalley), Folarin, Tutuola's

Index

Humanity of Tutuola's view of mankind, 126–128

Humor in the romances, from hyperbole, 124; from situation, 125–126; from traditional sources, 123–124; from Tutuola's wild fancy, 123

Hypocrisy of westerners who ridicule Africans for their failures and atrocities and ignore the failures and atrocities of the West, 90

Iron, God of (Ogun), in *Ajaiyi and His Inherited Poverty*, ix

King's "amputy" queen episode in *My Life in the Bush of Ghosts*, compared with analogue in Itayemi-Gurrey collection of West African folk tales, 57

Language of Tutuola's romances, its characteristics, x, 96, 99; as described by critics, 97–98; its oral quality, 98; representative samples, 99–100

Literary powers of Tutuola, summary of, 128

Literary standards, as only standards for judging fairly the romances of Tutuola, 95

Magic food-producing egg in *The Palm-Wine Drinkard*, compared with analogues in the Itayemi-Gurrey and the Barker-Sinclair collections of West African folk tales, 56

Magic transformations and other marvels, in *Ajaiyi and His Inherited Poverty*, x; in *The Brave African Huntress*, 72; in *Feather Woman of the Jungle*, 72–73; in *My Life in the Bush of Ghosts*, 71–72; in *The Palm-Wine Drinkard*, 71; in *Simbi and the Satyr of the Dark Jungle*, 72

Mbari Club, artists' club in Ibadan of which Tutuola is a (self-effacing) charter member, 22

Memorability of the incidents in the romances (with illustrations), 119

Methodist bishop of the Bush of Ghosts, a syncretic episode, 80–81

Monsters in Tutuola's works, considered as reflecting a pious Christian's view of the old Yoruba deities, 78; considered as possible Jungian archetypes, 77–78

Monsters, ogres and ogresses, in *Ajaiyi and His Inherited Poverty*, ix–x; in *The Brave African Huntress*, 75; in *Feather Woman of the Jungle*, 75–76; in *My Life in the Bush of Ghosts*, 74; in *The Palm-Wine Drinkard*, 73–74; in *Simbi and the Satyr of the Dark Jungle*, 72; vitality of these "unrealistic" characters, 73

Moore, Gerald, on Campbell's heroic monomyth pattern as it appears in *The Palm-Wine Drinkard*, *My Life in the Bush of Ghosts*, and *Simbi and the Satyr of the Dark Jungle*, 48–50; on Tutuola as a visionary, like Bunyan, 44

Mornu, F. O., Tutuola's Ibo employer and benefactor in Abeokuta and Lagos, 17–18

Mphahlele, Ezekiel, denies that pidgin, nonstandard English, or the experimental English of Okara and Sutherland have any future in African literature, 112–113

My Life in the Bush of Ghosts, plot summary of, 27; see also Characterization, Plot management, Point of view, and Romance quest

Narrative progression, lack of sense of, in Tutuola's romances, 51

Nwankwo, Nkem, idiomatic English of his novel *Danda*, 115

Nzekwu, Onuora, idiomatic English of his novels, 114–115

Odara, monstrous giant in *The Brave African Huntress*, 75

Old African, pre-contact atmosphere of the romances, 69–70

Originality, as it applies to the work of a folk artist working with folk tales, 53